HURON PUBLIC LIBRARY
333 WILLIAMS STREET
HURON, OHIO 44839

Chocolate Desserts
to die for!

Chocolate Desserts to die for!

Bev Shaffer

Food Photography and Food Styling by
John R. Shaffer

PELICAN PUBLISHING COMPANY
Gretna 2013

Copyright © 2013
By Bev Shaffer

Photographs copyright © 2013
By John R. Shaffer
All rights reserved

The word "Pelican" and the depiction of a pelican are trademarks of Pelican Publishing Company, Inc., and are registered in the U.S. Patent and Trademark Office.

Library of Congress Cataloging-in-Publication Data

Shaffer, Bev, 1951-
  Chocolate desserts to die for! / by Bev Shaffer ; food photography and food styling by John R. Shaffer.
       pages cm
  Includes index.
    ISBN 978-1-4556-1700-5 (hardcover : alk. paper) — ISBN 978-1-4556-1701-2 (e-book) 1. Chocolate desserts. 2. Cooking (Chocolate) 3. Chocolate. I. Shaffer, John R. II. Title.
  TX767.C5S46 2013
   641.86—dc23
                                                         2012049452

Printed in China

Published by Pelican Publishing Company, Inc.
1000 Burmaster Street, Gretna, Louisiana 70053

Your hand and your mouth agreed many years ago that, as far as chocolate is concerned, there is no need to involve your brain.
—Dave Barry

CONTENTS

Acknowledgments: Ready, Set, Chocolate! 9
Introduction: Carpe Chocolate! 10
Chocolate Trivia and a Brief History of Chocolate, in the Event
   That You're on a Quiz Show (You're Welcome) 11
Chocolate Trends: Know the Modern Playing Field 14
Finding a Favorite: Time for a Chocolate Tasting! 17
Know Your Chocolate 19
Chocolate Baking Tips 23
Comfort Chocolate 29
Chocolate Pairings 69
It's a Party! 107
Chocolate Gifts 143
Elegant Chocolate Desserts 173
Celebrate with Chef Bev Shaffer: Creating a Chocolate
   Dessert Buffet 219
Bibliography 221
Index 223

ACKNOWLEDGMENTS: READY, SET, CHOCOLATE!

All you need is love. But a little chocolate now and then doesn't hurt.
—Charles M. Schulz

Thank you to everyone who had a hand in helping make this book and its contents—ideas for rich, indulgent, chocolaty special delights, those little luxuries that keep people happy—a reality.

In particular, thank you to:

My husband, friend, photographer, food stylist, tester, tester-coordinator, delivery man, short-order cook, and early morning/late night biggest supporter, John. He brought this book to life with his chocolate photos (to die for!), photos that always make people want to get out their ingredients and cook.

Thanks to my chocolate-dessert testers, a willing group of fantastic ladies who shared my calories, oohs, aahs, and mishaps. They each took on a collection of recipes—some easy, some difficult, some perfect, some not—and agreed, on their own time, to recreate them and make comments. Special thanks go to: Vickie Getz, Annette Felton, Lisa Ann Ferring Mandel, Barbara Cumming, Tammy Bradfield, and Sarah Warnke.

Warm thanks to everyone at Pelican Publishing Company—from the editorial department to the warehouse staff to the sales team to the office staff to the production department to the publicists—for embracing this (and my other cookbooks) and then lavishing it with extraordinary attention.

Special thanks to the following chocolatiers and manufacturers who have graciously supported my efforts in so many ways. The quality of their products made testing such a joy. In no particular order, they are: Guittard Chocolate Company, a family-owned, US company established not long after the California gold rush; Chocolates El Rey, Venezuelan chocolates from the source; Organic Valley, organic and farmer-owned dairy products; Florida Crystals, organic and natural sugars made from one hundred percent sun-sweetened sugarcane; Wholesome Sweeteners, Fair Trade Certified organic and natural sugars, syrups, and nectars; Bob's Red Mill, whole grain foods for every meal of the day; and Anolon SureGrip Bakeware, heavy duty, nonstick bakeware that's a breeze to clean.

I hope that you will enjoy creating from this, my newest collection of recipes, and take pleasure in sharing these delicious, homemade indulgences with friends and family.

INTRODUCTION: CARPE CHOCOLATE!

My passion for chocolate has grown and flourished over the years. Why? Because of its taste, plain and simple. I'm a fan of the variety of its many-splendored flavors, ranging from the bite of extra bittersweet to the mellowness of a quality, creamy milk chocolate.

I've been captured in the web of chocolate's intrigue, and too much is never enough. I enjoy indulging in rich, gooey confections—biting into one of my brownie-filled cookies, a sea salt-encrusted truffle, or a slice of deep, dark chocolate cake with white chocolate curls is the best kind of treat. In addition, I enjoy pairing chocolate concoctions with its classic, complementary cousins—peanut butter, caramel, mint, raspberry, sea salt, coffee, and vanilla—to name just a few.

People around the world have consumed chocolate for centuries, claiming both psychological and health benefits. Is chocolate a cure-all? Whether it is or is not an ultimate panacea, here are just some of my reasons why it's good to indulge:

- Chocolate makes people smile. Just the sight of it can evoke a grin. Many women rank chocolate as the most smile-worthy sight, edging out loved ones and other smiling people! Chocolate contains phenethylamine, a naturally occurring substance in the body believed to help ward off the blues.
- It might help to strengthen eyesight. Flavonols—antioxidants present in dark chocolate but absent in white chocolate—could improve vision.
- Chocolate is a diet food! Preliminary findings from a US chocolate producer suggest that natural cocoa, which has more flavonols than Dutch-processed cocoa, may prevent some fats and starches in other foods from being absorbed. More definitive research is needed . . . and I would happily volunteer as a test subject. Wouldn't you?

Chocolate holds a special place for me as a chef. It is unique among foods, used as an ingredient, a flavoring, and a foodstuff in its own right. Eating a small piece of chocolate is a heavenly experience—cocoa butter melts at body temperature, so there is always the chance to experience that moment when the chocolate is no longer solid but not yet liquid. This sensation is irresistible to me (and to many other chocolate lovers). If you have melted chocolate on your hands, you're eating it too slowly!

But wait—there's more. Chocolate's aroma, its ability to create taste memories, and its indescribably rich flavor all combine to make it a food that most people cannot resist—and really, why should we?

CHOCOLATE TRIVIA AND A BRIEF HISTORY OF CHOCOLATE, IN THE EVENT THAT YOU'RE ON A QUIZ SHOW (YOU'RE WELCOME)

Do you think you know everything there is to know about chocolate? Here is some trivia that might astound both you and your friends (the answers are at the end of this section—but no cheating!):

1. The average cacao pod contains about how many seeds?
   1. 30 to 50
   2. 100 to 200
   3. 1,000 to 2,000
2. Wild cacao trees grow up to how many feet tall beneath a canopy of taller trees?
   1. 30 feet tall
   2. 75 feet tall
   3. 100 feet tall
3. Chocolate syrup was used to represent what in Alfred Hitchcock's movie *Psycho*'s 45-second shower scene that took 7 days to shoot?
4. True or False. American and Russian space flights have always included chocolate.

Chocolate appears in our everyday lives in a variety of drinks, a multitude of desserts, countless candy bars, and more. But what, exactly, is chocolate's history—its family tree?

We generally associate chocolate with a sweet candy created during modern times. In truth, the tasty secret of the cacao tree was discovered more than two thousand years ago in the tropical rainforests of the Americas. The pods of this tree contain the seeds that are processed into chocolate. The story of how chocolate grew from a local Mesoamerican beverage into a global sweet encompasses many cultures and many continents; it is truly a universal food.

Mesoamerica is a cultural region extending approximately from today's central Mexico to Honduras and Nicaragua. It is also the area within which a number of pre-Columbian societies flourished before the Spanish colonization of the Americas in the fifteenth and sixteenth centuries.

The first peoples known to have made chocolate were the ancient societies of Mexico and Central America from 250 to 900 AD. These people, including the Maya and the Aztecs, mixed ground cacao seeds with various seasonings (such as chilies) to make a bitter but beloved beverage. This beverage was often limited to royalty. Chocolate played a role in both Maya and Aztec royal and religious events. To the Aztecs, chocolate was a luxury, a drink for warriors and nobility and used in rituals and ceremonies. They also used cacao seeds as money. In fact, the seeds were so valuable that it is believed that dishonest merchants made counterfeits.

The Spanish, searching for gold in the New World, found cacao instead. Conquest of the Aztecs made it possible to export chocolate back to Europe, where it quickly became a court favorite. By the 1600s, the love of chocolate spread through the rest of Europe. Before long, the English, Dutch, and French were so enamored of chocolate that they set out to colonize cacao-growing lands of their own. Because of the desire for profit and product, the chocolate trade was built on a system of forced labor and slavery.

The introduction of chocolate created myths about its benefits. Some of the earliest European cocoa-makers were apothecaries seeking medicinal uses of the plant. Chocolate's reputation as an aphrodisiac flourished in the French courts. Casanova was reputed to have used chocolate with champagne to seduce the ladies. In Italy, chocolate was the preferred drink of the Cardinals—they even had it delivered inside the Vatican while they were electing a new Pope.

By the mid-1700s, the blossoming Industrial Revolution saw the emergence of innovations that changed the future of chocolate. New machinery made it possible to create solid chocolate and mass-produce it at a fraction of its original cost. These innovations included the following notable discoveries.

In 1776, a Frenchman named Doret invented a hydraulic machine that ground cacao seeds into a paste. Not long afterward, it was replaced by the steam engine, which made it even easier to produce large amounts of chocolate.

In 1828, a Dutch chemist, Coenraad Johannes van Houten, invented the cocoa press, which extracted cocoa butter from chocolate, leaving the powder we call cocoa.

In the 1870s in Switzerland, Daniel Peter and Henri Nestlé developed the world's first milk chocolate bar using Nestlé's creation, powdered milk.

In 1879, Rodolphe Lindt invented a machine that churned a paste squeezed from cocoa seeds into a smooth blend, giving chocolate a new, mellow texture. Today, that process is known as conching.

In 1893, Pennsylvania confectioner Milton Hershey discovered chocolate pressing equipment at the World's Columbian Exposition in Chicago. He bought the machinery, built a chocolate factory and town in the hills of southern Pennsylvania, and became the "Henry Ford of chocolate makers." For the first time, the general public could afford this treat.

So, who eats chocolate today? Although the largest percentage of chocolate is grown on the Ivory Coast of Africa, it is mostly exported. Chocolate features in African dishes very rarely. Chocolate's popularity is growing in China and Japan, but comparatively there is little chocolate culture in Asia. Mexicans consume chocolate more as a traditional drink and as a spice than as a candy. They use it to make one variety of the sauce *mole* and offer chocolate drinks at many social gatherings. Americans devour chocolate at an average of 12 pounds per person per year. Europeans have enjoyed it since the late 1700s; they consume nearly 12 million pounds of chocolate per year.

Today, 15 of the 16 leading per capita chocolate-consuming countries are located in Europe, with Switzerland leading the pack.

Trivia Answers: 1. 30 to 50 almond-sized seeds, enough to make about 7 milk chocolate candy bars. 2. 30 feet tall. The canopy of trees protects cacao from the intense tropical sun, wind damage, and moisture loss. 3. Blood. 4. True.

CHOCOLATE TRENDS: KNOW THE MODERN PLAYING FIELD

TREND #1: THE NUMBERS GAME

The choices used to be straightforward: dark, milk, or white; sweet, semisweet, or bittersweet. Today, however, you need to sort your choices: do you want 47 percent cocoa content, 73 percent, or an ultrapure 99 percent?

How cacao content is calculated: Cacao content refers to the total amount of cocoa (cocoa solids plus cocoa butter) in the chocolate. Don't be misled by just the numbers—there are so many factors that contribute to quality chocolate. Rely on what tastes best to you.

Most chocolate is a simple confection, a blend of cacao products, sugar, and milk solids. The ratio of the blend affects taste, texture, and its reaction in baking. The label should indicate how much of that ratio is composed of cacao.

A higher percentage of cacao, however, does not guarantee a more intense flavor, because cacao percentages represent a tally of cocoa solids (from which chocolate gets its flavor) and cocoa butter (which imparts chocolate's lush mouth feel, but no real flavor). So, while different chocolates may have the same percent of total cacao, they could contain different ratios of solids and butter, which would dramatically influence taste and texture. In addition, higher percentages do not necessarily indicate higher quality. Taste is influenced more by the origin, blend, and roasting of the beans.

Fast forward, and soon you'll be shopping for chocolate by exploring the origin and variety of beans, much like coffee.

TREND #2: ORIGIN MATTERS

The Fair Trade label guarantees that farmers are paid a fair price for their crop, improving the families' quality of life and the stability of the local economy. Though not every fairly traded product is organic, many support ecologically sustainable farming practices that aim to protect the environment, the farming community, and consumers from dangerous chemicals.

TREND #3: PERFECT PAIRINGS

Of course, there are the classics—raspberries, strawberries, marshmallow, peanut butter, lavender. All of these enhance the complexity and flavor of sweet chocolate.

However, chocolate also has a savory side—the most common flavor profiles associated with savory chocolate dishes are smoky and spicy. Cayenne and chili peppers are commonly used to add heat, while chipotle, paprika, and cumin are used to add smokiness. Cinnamon is an excellent spice for chocolate because it imparts a hint of warm, earthy sweetness. The goal of using chocolate in a main dish is to keep it from being too sweet. Cocoa powder and unsweetened chocolate are not sweet at all and have more of a true chocolate quality, so you want to bring out these natural flavors instead of making them reminiscent of the sweet side of chocolate that we know and love.

TREND #4: CHOCOLATE TASTINGS

Chocolate tastings, similar to wine tastings, are becoming more popular and frequent as cultural and social interest in chocolate grows. At tastings, certain aspects of chocolate are noted and appreciated.

Flavor: Like the grapes used to make wine, the beans used to make chocolate have their own distinctive flavors, as shaped by the soil, climate, and location where the varietals are grown. Chocolate makers play with the cocoa beans to nurture and develop nuanced flavors during processing. You might note a dark, roasted flavor typical of a very strong coffee in a product processed at a high temperature. Other chocolates might accentuate nutty notes or highlight an aromatic, fruity flavor of the beans.

Conching: Conching is a specific processing technique used to develop the cocoa flavor. It combines heat and agitation to drive off any unwanted acidic or astringent tastes while developing pleasant notes such as caramel. You might detect unappealing moldy, woody, meaty, or salty flavors in lesser quality chocolate, usually a result of poor-quality beans or inferior processing.

Melt: Melt describes the feeling of a piece of chocolate when you press it against the roof of your mouth. A lesser chocolate may leave a thick, waxy coating or have a grainy texture. The cocoa solids in premium chocolate are ground more finely to reduce the particle size so that the tongue can't detect individual sugar crystals. That extra attention is what creates the silky, smooth melt of a high-quality product.

Linger: Linger is the lasting effect of the chocolate in your mouth after you swallow it. Ideally, the beautiful chocolate flavor with which you start should have the same flavor with which you end. High quality chocolate has one pleasant, uniform bouquet from start to finish, without off notes or any harsh, sugary sweetness at the end.

Your ability to differentiate subtle flavor variations in chocolate depends both on your taste buds and experience. The more chocolate you taste, the more notes you will be able to pick up. What better excuse to eat more chocolate?

DEVELOPING TRENDS

- Consumers are sourcing single-origin premium chocolate. These bars have distinguishable, bold flavors due to one type of bean as opposed to a blend of beans.
- Spreadable chocolate: Nutella has led the way, and other creamy concoctions have followed.
- Chocolate dishes from Africa? The Phillipines? We've already had (and enjoyed!) Mexican mole. American chefs are crafting dishes with chocolate rubs and nose-to-tail pork specialties. You name it, we're cooking it!
- Gendered chocolates: on average, women prefer darker, more intense chocolate flavors, while men enjoy sweeter, lighter tastes.
- Alcohol and chocolate: chocolate craft beer, anyone?

FINDING A FAVORITE: TIME FOR A CHOCOLATE TASTING!

The first step to finding the perfect chocolate for baking and cooking is finding one that you enjoy eating straight out of the package. While many of the nuances of flavor and texture might get lost in cooking, you want to use a chocolate whose general flavor profile is very pleasing to you—it will make your creations even more irresistible.

Get started by choosing a few chocolates that have something in common: they all may be in the same price range or from the same country, or they all may have the same cocoa percentage. It is much easier to evaluate their differences if they have some unifying qualities, too.

Tasting chocolate is similar to tasting wine. By focusing on several different components, you can center your senses and understand the character of what you taste and what you enjoy in a piece of chocolate.

Here is the most traditional tasting method:
- Put a tiny piece of chocolate in your mouth, chew it, then stop and allow it to melt.
- Concentrate on what you feel. Note if there are any changes in flavor and what your tongue feels.
- Look for different flavors (for example, floral notes, fruity overtones, or leathery and smoky profiles):
    - Do you recognize them?
    - Do they evolve over time?
    - Do they interact with each other, or do they seem to come in separate phases? Is one more pleasant and clear than the others, or are they muddled together?
    - Do you feel any bitterness, acidity, or astringency? Do you find it mild or severe?
- A good chocolate has three distinct phases. Try to distinguish between:
    - what you feel in a few seconds,
    - what you feel while it slowly melts, and
    - what you feel once you have swallowed. This last phase is called the "end of mouth."
- Now score the chocolate you just tasted globally out of ten.

Try doing the following exercise with a square of chocolate. Consider this your tasting checklist:

- Look at it. What do you see? What is its color? Shine? Texture? Is there any blooming or discoloration? Break a piece and look at the interior. How does the broken surface look: smooth or rough? Bubbly? Sticky?
- Touch it. What do you feel? How does the texture of the surface compare with the touch of the interior?
- Listen to it. What do you hear as you snap a square in half? A loud crack? A soft break?
- Smell it. What other flavors do you find?
- Taste it. Analyze the texture. Notice its effect on your tongue. How does it feel in your mouth? As you chew? As it melts?

With these guidelines, you will be on your way to finding your perfect piece of chocolate. Sit back, relax, and let the tasting begin!

KNOW YOUR CHOCOLATE

Chocolate makes what might have been an ordinary meal, or an ordinary day, memorable!

—Bev Shaffer

THE VARIETIES

By the time chocolate reaches your kitchen, it has already undergone a complex process of transformation, from the raw cacao bean to the dark, smooth substance we know as chocolate.

Unlike sugar, which had a long history of use before mechanization, chocolate's comparatively recent usage in confectionary is closely linked to developments in manufacturing processes.

Cocoa nibs are tiny pieces of roasted cocoa beans that can be used as a crunchy ingredient much as you'd use roasted nuts. Strongly flavored, they are sometimes slightly bitter but appealingly chocolaty.

Chocolate liquor, a dark, pasty liquid made by grinding the nibs extracted from dried, fermented, and roasted cacao beans, is pure unsweetened chocolate—the base ingredient for all other processed chocolates.

About 55 percent of chocolate liquor is *cocoa butter,* a natural fat responsible for chocolate's unique texture. Its melting point is close to body temperature, which explains why chocolate melts smoothly in your mouth but stays solid and shelf stable at room temperature. Suspended in the cocoa butter are particles of ground cocoa solids, which carry the flavor we associate with chocolate.

Unsweetened chocolate contains no sugar. It is more or less the chocolate liquor that has been cooled and formed into bars.

Cocoa powder is the result of chocolate liquor fed through a press to remove all but 10 percent to 24 percent of the cocoa butter. So, ounce for ounce, cocoa powder packs a bigger punch of chocolate flavor, because you're getting more cocoa solids and less cocoa butter. Cocoa powder is sold plain (natural or Dutch process) to be used in baking, or, when mixed with other ingredients such as milk powder and sugar, forms an instant cocoa mix. It should be stored in an airtight container in a cool, dark place.

Dutch-processed cocoa is chocolate that has gone through a different treatment to make it commercially palatable. Once the chocolate liquor is dried, the hardened mass is ground into a powder known as unsweetened cocoa. Then, the chocolate is treated with an alkali, which helps neutralize cocoa's natural acidity. This method, called dutching, was introduced in 1828 by a Dutch chemist named Coenraad Johannes van Houten. By reducing the cocoa's acidity, dutching eliminates the sharpness that can overwhelm other aspects of the cocoa's flavor. It also mixes more easily with water.

White chocolate is technically not chocolate, because it contains no cocoa solids or chocolate liquor. It is made with cocoa butter (the fat from cocoa beans), sugar, and milk and usually contains natural vanilla or vanillin, an artificial flavoring. White chocolate has a quick, even melt and creamy texture. When you buy white chocolate, make sure that cocoa butter is on and near the beginning of the list of ingredients on the label.

Milk chocolate is what is most often used in candy bars and must contain at least 10 percent chocolate liquor and 12 percent dry milk solids. In Europe, milk chocolate must contain 30 percent chocolate liquor and 18 percent dry milk solids.

Sweet chocolate—milk chocolate without the milk—is also referred to as *sweet dark chocolate*. While it must contain at least 15 percent chocolate liquor, it is often more than 60 percent sugar.

Bittersweet, or *semisweet chocolate,* is often an overlapping category, with semisweet giving a slightly sweeter result. Practically speaking, there is no difference between the two. By FDA standards, both chocolates must contain at least 35 percent chocolate liquor (unsweetened chocolate). After this requirement is met, the individual manufacturers can add more chocolate liquor as well as sugar, additional cocoa butter, milk solids, lecithin (for preserving), and flavorings, such as vanilla. (Note that the addition of milk solids does not make these chocolates milk chocolate. It is sometimes added in very small amounts as a way to smooth out the texture.)

SPOTTING SUPERIOR CHOCOLATE

Here's a brief how-to in your quest to hunt down an incredible piece of chocolate.
- flavor: should be well balanced, not too bitter or too sweet
- appearance: should be shiny and evenly colored
- aroma: should be rich and flavorful, not burned, musky, or chemical in scent
- snap: should break firmly and cleanly, not crumble or splinter
- texture/mouth feel: should be smooth and creamy, not waxy or gritty
- aftertaste: should linger pleasantly on your tongue

VARIATIONS ON A CHOCOLATE THEME

If you want to infuse your cooking with a little chocolate variety, try baking with the specialty chips available—callets, pearls, or chocolate drops.

Chocolate extract is perfect for that change of pace to add a hint of chocolate flavor to anything from crème anglaise to whipped cream or top notes of sauces, chili, and other spicy foods. It's neither sweet nor milky and offers the full depth of dark chocolate.

GLORIOUS GARNISHES

Garnishes of chocolate pack a double punch: they not only taste delicious but also look great! Chocolate can be cut out, grated, shaved, curled, or chopped to make garnishes that give a touch of luxury and elegance to any dessert. For best results, handle the chocolate as little as possible and be sure your utensils are absolutely dry.

Chocolate confetti: Shavings of chocolate add a jaunty look to an iced cake. Drag a vegetable peeler across a thick block of chocolate and collect the shavings on a sheet of parchment paper.

Chocolate curls: Make these as you would the confetti, but first warm the chocolate slightly (microwave in five-second jolts). Apply pressure with a vegetable peeler to get longer strips that will curl naturally. Let them fall in a single layer onto a piece of parchment paper. Re-warm the block of chocolate as necessary.

Decorative drizzle: To give baked goods that finishing touch, improvise a piping bag from a small re-sealable plastic bag. Scrape melted chocolate into the bag, seal it, and gather the chocolate into one corner. Snip off a small bit of the tip and you're ready to drizzle.

Chocolate shapes: Spread melted chocolate about 1/8-inch thick on waxed paper or parchment paper. Chill until it is no longer soft but not yet hard. Cut shapes with a decorative cookie cutter or sharp knife. Chill cutouts until you are ready to use them.

Chocolate dipping: What doesn't look (and taste) better dipped in a little chocolate? Use tempered chocolate for professional-looking results; however, if you're going to chill or freeze the dipped item, tempering (stabilizing the chocolate) is less important. Be sure the item is dry and at room temperature. Use tweezers, forks, or special dipping tools to make your life easier. Dip only halfway to allow the item's original color and texture to contrast with the chocolate. (Also, it keeps your fingers clean.) Be sure to set the dipped items on parchment-lined baking sheets, and allow the chocolate to set for one to two hours.

CHOOSING CHOCOLATE FOR GANACHE

In cooking, you should use only a wine that you would drink, and the same holds true for chocolate. Chocolate is one of only two basic ingredients in ganache, so use only a chocolate that's good enough to eat straight from the package.

A chocolate that is between 55 percent and 60 percent chocolate liquor is generally a good choice for ganache. Rich and moderately sweet without a strong bitter edge, it will produce consistent results. Ganache made with higher-percentage chocolate may be less stable and prone to curdling.

Don't cut corners by using chocolate chips for ganache. They often contain added ingredients that help them hold their shape when baked, which translates into an overly thick, viscous ganache.

Natural, unsweetened cocoa powder with all its rich, deep, dark flavors.

CHOCOLATE BAKING TIPS

STORING CHOCOLATE

Never store chocolate in the refrigerator or freezer, as cocoa butter can easily pick up flavors from other foods. If chocolate is exposed to rapid changes in humidity or temperature, sugar or fat may dissolve and migrate, discoloring the surface. This cosmetic alternation, or bloom, is not harmful—bloomed chocolate is safe both to eat and cook. Always wrap chocolate tightly in plastic and store it in a cool, dry place.

GETTING AN EDGE ON CHOPPING CHOCOLATE

Whether you're chopping chocolate to melt it or to create chunks for adding to a recipe, you need to chop it evenly and quickly.

For easy cleanup, first line a rimmed baking sheet with parchment paper to catch the inevitable flying shards of chocolate. Put your cutting board on top of the parchment paper. When you're finished, you will be able to use the paper to easily gather the extra shards.

Serrated knives are great for chopping chocolate, especially when you want evenly sized chunks for cookies. The serrations bite down into the chocolate to keep the blade from slipping, and since you don't have to press down as hard, the chocolate won't break into as many tiny pieces.

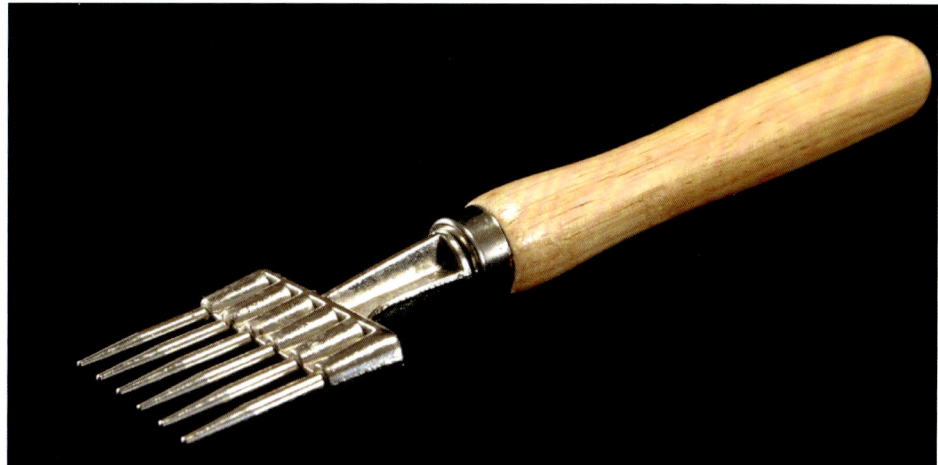

A chocolate chipper is my go-to gadget when chopping chocolate.

Another classic way to chop large blocks of chocolate is with a "chocolate chipper." Poke the chipper into the block and push down with both hands. The prongs will pierce the chocolate at even intervals and separate it into easy-to-use pieces.

THE SCOOP ON MELTING CHOCOLATE

Melting chocolate to use as a baking ingredient requires gentle heat. Chocolate that is overheated may scorch, lose flavor, or turn coarse and grainy. Stir melting chocolate after it has begun to liquefy. Because of the sensitivity of milk solids to heat, milk and white chocolates should be chopped finely, melted with minimal heat and stirred almost constantly during melting. White chocolate contains high percentages of both cocoa butter and milk solids, so it is the most temperature-sensitive of the chocolates. Be careful when you melt it—it burns easily, so again, use very low heat. In addition, with too much heat, the milk solids can coagulate, leaving tiny lumps in the chocolate. Be sure to use a water bath or a very low power setting on the microwave (details below). Dark chocolate needs to be stirred infrequently while melting.

Stovetop: Place coarsely chopped chocolate in the top of a double boiler over hot—not simmering or boiling—water. Let the heat melt the chocolate, stirring until smooth. When the chocolate is ready, remove the top part of the double boiler and wipe moisture off of the bottom of the pot carefully and gently with a dry cloth, being careful that you allow no steam or water droplets to get into the melted chocolate.

Alternately, put chopped chocolate in a heatproof bowl that fits snugly over a pot of barely simmering water (or put the bowl directly in a wide, shallow skillet of barely simmering water). Stir occasionally until the chocolate is melted and smooth; remove it from the heat. Be careful not to let water come in contact with the chocolate, and be sure the bowl and spoon or spatula are perfectly dry.

Microwave Oven: Place coarsely chopped chocolate in a microwave-safe container and microwave the chocolate on medium (50 percent power) for 1½ minutes. Remove the container from the microwave and stir the chocolate. Continue heating until melted, stirring once every additional minute, until completely smooth. Stir milk and white chocolate after about 1½ additional minutes. Because of their milk proteins, they need to be stirred sooner than dark chocolate. (If overheated, these chocolates become grainy and clumpy.)

When melting in a microwave oven, remember that chocolate retains its shape as it melts, so don't rely on appearance alone. The only way to know if it is fully melted is to stir it.

Just what is seized chocolate? We love chocolate, but it does have one annoying habit: it can seize while you're melting it if any amount of moisture mixes with the chocolate. Instead of a smooth, glossy, melted chocolate bliss, you have on your hands a grainy, matte, clumpy mess. Why? And how can you fix it?

Chocolate is composed of fine, dry particles (cocoa and sugar) in rich fat (cocoa butter). If a few drops of water—or even a bit of steam—should get stirred into melted chocolate, the dry cocoa and sugar particles will clump together.

You can usually fix seized chocolate by whisking in more water, which will provide enough liquid to wet all of the seized particles and smooth the chocolate. However, this may change the proportions in your recipe, so pay attention to what other liquids and proportions you need.

SOME SIMPLE RULES YOU REALLY *SHOULD* REMEMBER . . .

Chefs refer to it as *mise en place* (everything in place). Bottom line: get organized before you begin to bake or cook. Also, always read through a

The chocolate trifecta: milk, white, and bittersweet!

recipe before you begin preparing it! You want to make sure that you know what you're doing.

- Do anything that needs special handling first, such as softening cream cheese or butter, chopping nuts or fruit, or zesting a lemon.
- Properly measure all ingredients, using dry and liquid measuring cups where appropriate.
- Follow the recipe! After a successful venture, you can explore the unknown and improvise. For starters, though, stick to what has already been tried and true.
- Every ingredient matters—so don't substitute margarine if the recipe calls for unsalted butter. Don't substitute ingredients (unless you know how to counter the properties that they bring to the recipe).
- Let the oven preheat for ten to fifteen minutes before putting anything in it.
- Be patient. Follow the steps. Breathe. Let the final product chill or rest, and then enjoy!
- Smile. Have fun. It's *chocolate*—enjoy the experience.

CHOCOLATE DESSERTS
to die for!

COMFORT CHOCOLATE

An easy-to-work-with pastry dough puts this Chocolate Nut Tart on the top of your to-do list!

In the mood for something soothing? Need to cuddle up with a good dessert? These recipes—some familiar, some not—all call upon our fond comfort-food memories with spoonfuls and forkfuls of *yum!*

Chocolate Nut Tart

Loaded with flavorful nuts and deep dark chocolate, this tart is a winner for a comforting dessert with style.

PASTRY DOUGH

- 2 cups unbleached, all-purpose flour
- ⅔ cup confectioners' sugar, sifted
- ⅔ cup unsalted butter, cold, cut into pieces
- 2 large egg yolks

FILLING

- 1 cup walnut pieces, lightly toasted
- 1 cup pecan pieces, lightly toasted
- 3 large eggs, beaten
- 1 cup light brown sugar, firmly packed
- 1 cup evaporated milk
- 1 tsp. vanilla extract
- ¼ cup unsalted butter, melted and cooled
- 10 oz. bittersweet chocolate, melted and slightly cooled

For the Pastry: Pulse the flour, confectioners' sugar and butter in a food processor until mixture resembles coarse crumbs. Add egg yolks and continue to pulse to form a dough.

Roll dough on a lightly floured board to form a large circle and gently place in an ungreased 11" tart pan with removable bottom. Carefully press dough into bottom and sides (crust will be thick). Trim away any excess dough, then chill in the refrigerator for 30 minutes to 1 hour until cold.

Heat oven to 350 degrees.

Prick dough all over with a fork, then gently place a sheet of foil on top of dough and weigh down with dried beans. Bake for 15 minutes.

Slowly and carefully remove beans and foil and return the pan to the oven for an additional 12 to 15 minutes or until pastry is a light golden color. Remove from the oven and set aside on a wire rack to cool.

Reduce oven to 325 degrees.

For the Filling: Mix together the walnuts, pecans, eggs, brown sugar, milk, vanilla, and butter in a large bowl. Stir in the melted chocolate.

Pour mixture into crust and return to the oven for 55 minutes to 1 hour or until set, lightly covering with foil if needed to prevent the tart from burning.

Allow to cool completely on a wire rack, then carefully remove the bottom of the tart pan. Cut into slices and serve. Yield: 8 to 10 servings.

Chocolate Cranberry Oat Cookies

Three chocolates and fresh cranberries? Your oatmeal cookies will never be the same!

1 cup unbleached, all-purpose flour
½ tsp. baking soda
½ tsp. ground cinnamon
¼ tsp. salt
½ cup plus 2 tbsp. unsalted butter, room temperature, cut into pieces
½ cup granulated sugar
½ cup light brown sugar, firmly packed
1 large egg
1 tsp. vanilla
1 cup old-fashioned rolled oats
½ cup semisweet or bittersweet chocolate chips
½ cup milk chocolate chips
½ cup white chocolate chips
½ cup fresh cranberries, coarsely chopped
2 oz. white chocolate, coarsely chopped, for garnish

Heat oven to 350 degrees. Line two large, rimmed baking sheets with parchment paper or silicone liners.

In a medium bowl, whisk together flour, baking soda, cinnamon, and salt.

In the large bowl of an electric mixer, beat the butter, granulated sugar, and brown sugar until smooth. Scrape down the edges of the bowl to incorporate all of the ingredients. Beat in the egg and vanilla.

Add flour mixture and oats to the sugar mixture, stirring until blended. Add the chocolate chips and cranberries.

Drop batter by rounded tablespoonful onto prepared baking sheets, about 2" apart. Bake for 12 to 16 minutes or until edges are lightly browned.

Cool on sheets 5 minutes, then remove and cool completely on wire racks.

Melt white chocolate just until smooth. Using a fork or small spoon, drizzle chocolate over cookies in a zigzag pattern. Let rest (if you can resist!) until chocolate sets, about 1 hour. Yield: 28 cookies.

Cranberries and chocolates in a delicate oatmeal cookie make for a rewarding combination.

Not My Momma's Rice Pudding with Cranberry Compote

To me, rice pudding is comfort food at its finest.

RICE PUDDING

4½ cups milk, whole or 2%
⅔ cup basmati or other long grain white rice
⅔ cup granulated sugar
1 tbsp. vanilla extract
¼ tsp. salt
2 large egg yolks
3 tbsp. heavy whipping cream
4 oz. white chocolate, coarsely chopped
1 tbsp. orange zest

CRANBERRY COMPOTE

1 cup cranberry juice cocktail
½ cup fresh cranberries, coarsely chopped
1 cup dried cranberries, coarsely chopped
¼ tsp. vanilla extract

Bev's Bites

Compote may be prepared 2 days ahead and kept covered and refrigerated until ready to use.

Leftover compote? Stir into plain yogurt for a refreshing snack.

For the Rice Pudding: In a large saucepan, combine the milk, rice, sugar, vanilla, and salt. Cook over medium-low heat, stirring often, until mixture thickens and rice is very tender, about 1 hour.

Reduce heat to low. Whisk the egg yolks and cream in a small bowl, then gradually whisk in ½ cup of the rice mixture until blended. Return this mixture to the saucepan and cook for 2 minutes, stirring constantly (do not boil). Remove saucepan from heat.

Add white chocolate and stir until melted. Stir in the orange zest until blended. Transfer pudding to a bowl; cover and chill until cold.

For the Cranberry Compote: In a small saucepan, combine the cranberry juice cocktail and fresh cranberries and bring to a boil. Boil gently for 10 minutes.

Add the dried cranberries and vanilla and return mixture to a boil, stirring occasionally. Cover and remove saucepan from the heat. Let mixture stand until almost all of the liquid has been absorbed, about 1 hour. Refrigerate until cold. Yield: 4-6 servings.

My rice pudding redux—complete with the sweet creaminess of white chocolate and the bright, tart flavors of a cranberry compote.

Gooey Caramel Pecan Brownies

A brownie with a crusty top and a sticky, gooey drizzle . . . prepare to indulge.

CARAMEL TOPPING

- 1 cup granulated sugar
- ¼ tsp. fresh lemon juice
- ¼ cup cold water
- ½ cup heavy whipping cream
- 3 tbsp. unsalted butter, cut into pieces
- 1 tsp. vanilla extract
- ¼ teaspoon salt

BROWNIES

- ¾ cup unsalted butter, room temperature, cut into pieces
- 4 oz. unsweetened chocolate, coarsely chopped
- 4 large eggs
- 1¾ cups granulated sugar
- 1½ tsp. vanilla extract
- ¼ tsp. salt
- ¾ cup unbleached, all-purpose flour
- ¼ cup unsweetened, natural cocoa powder, sifted
- 1½ cups pecans, coarsely chopped and lightly toasted

NUT GARNISH

- 3 oz. bittersweet chocolate, coarsely chopped
- 2 tbsp. heavy whipping cream
- ½ cup coarsely chopped pecans, lightly toasted

Bev's Bites

Once the caramel mixture begins to color, it will darken very quickly, so keep a watchful eye on it!

For the Caramel Topping: In a 2-quart saucepan, stir the sugar, lemon juice, and cold water. Brush down the sides of the pan with a pastry brush dipped in water to wash away any sugar crystals. Bring mixture to a boil over medium-high heat and cook, occasionally brushing down sides of the pan, until the mixture starts to color around the edges. Gently swirl the pan once to even out the color and prevent the sugar from burning in isolated spots. Continue to cook until the sugar turns medium amber.

Remove the pan from the heat and carefully add the cream—the mixture will bubble furiously. Once the bubbling has subsided, add the butter and gently whisk until completely melted. Whisk in the vanilla and salt, then set saucepan aside while mixing the brownies.

For the Brownies: Heat oven to 350 degrees. Lightly grease the bottom and sides of a 13" x 9" baking pan.

Melt the butter and chocolate in a medium saucepan over low heat, stirring constantly, until melted and smooth. Remove from heat and set aside.

In a large bowl, whisk the eggs until blended, then gradually—but vigorously—whisk in the sugar until well blended. Add the melted chocolate mixture, vanilla, and salt. Whisk in the flour and cocoa powder until blended.

Stir in the pecans. Scrape the batter into the prepared pan and smooth for an even top.

Bake for 18 to 20 minutes or until a toothpick inserted in the center comes out with just a few moist crumbs attached. Cool in pan on a wire rack for 5 minutes.

Pour the caramel topping over the brownies, using a spatula to spread it evenly over the entire top. Let the brownies cool on the rack for 45 minutes and then refrigerate until the caramel topping is set, at least 1 hour.

For the Nut Garnish: When ready to serve, combine the chocolate and heavy cream in a small saucepan over low heat and stir constantly until mixture is melted and smooth. Pour the chocolate into a small resealable plastic bag and seal; snip off the corner of the bag to make a small hole. Drizzle the chocolate over the brownies in a zigzag pattern and sprinkle the chopped pecans over the top. Refrigerate again until the chocolate is set, about 20 minutes.

Cut the brownies and serve chilled or at room temperature. Yield: 24 brownies.

Go ahead, lick the parchment paper when you're done. You know you want to.

Slice 'N Bake Chocolate Cookies

Also referred to as icebox cookies, these cookie rolls can be made ahead and stored for a slice-and-bake, easy-to-make, and keep-on-hand treat.

½ cup unsalted butter, room temperature
½ cup light brown sugar, firmly packed
⅓ cup granulated sugar
1 large egg
1 tsp. vanilla extract
2 oz. unsweetened chocolate, melted and cooled
1¾ cups unbleached, all-purpose flour, divided
½ tsp. baking soda
⅛ tsp. salt

Bev's Bites

The logs may be stored in a plastic bag and refrigerated for up to 1 week or frozen for up to 2 months.

Here are a few clever solutions for keeping your logs round. To keep them from flattening out on the bottom while it chills, try these ideas:

   Turn frequently. Put the logs on a level shelf or flat baking sheet in the refrigerator or freezer and turn each log every 15 minutes for the first hour. As the logs chill, the bottoms will flatten from the weight of the dough. To correct this, remold the logs by rolling them back and forth a few times on the countertop.

   Use a cradle. If you happen to have a baguette pan, it makes a perfect cradle for chilling logs of dough. If you don't, save an empty paper towel roll and cut in half lengthwise to make two cardboard troughs with rounded bottoms. Place a log in each half for chilling. For both of these methods, after the logs have chilled for 15 to 20 minutes, turn them over once and chill until firm.

In the large bowl of an electric mixer, beat the butter until light and fluffy. Scrape down the sides of the bowl.

Add the brown sugar and granulated sugar and beat until well blended. Scrape down the sides of the bowl, then add the egg and vanilla and beat until well blended.

Beat in the melted chocolate, then add ¾ cup of the flour along with the baking soda and salt.

Stir in by hand the remaining 1 cup of flour to make a soft dough.

Divide the dough in half and wrap each half in waxed paper or plastic wrap. Shape into a 6"-long log. Refrigerate until firm.

Heat the oven to 350 degrees.

Using a thin knife, slice each log into pieces ⅛" to ¼" thick. Arrange the cookies 1" apart on parchment paper or silicone lined cookie sheets and bake for 10 to 15 minutes or until lightly golden around the edges. Yield: 4½ dozen cookies.

A Comforting Collection of Sauces
Try them all and pick your fave!

GOOEY FUDGE SAUCE

½ cup heavy whipping cream
4 tbsp. unsalted butter, cut into pieces
½ cup light brown sugar, firmly packed
¼ cup granulated sugar
Pinch of salt
½ cup unsweetened cocoa powder, sifted
½ tsp. vanilla extract

SMOOTH AND SILKY FUDGE SAUCE

4 oz. bittersweet chocolate, coarsely chopped
⅓ cup unsalted butter, cut into pieces
1⅓ cups confectioners' sugar, sifted
¾ cup half-and-half
1 tsp. vanilla extract

BEV'S HOT FUDGE SAUCE

⅓ cup heavy whipping cream
3 tbsp. light corn syrup
3 tbsp. light brown sugar, firmly packed
2 tbsp. unsweetened cocoa powder, sifted
¼ tsp. salt
3½ oz. bittersweet chocolate, coarsely chopped
½ tsp. vanilla extract

Bev's Bites

Store any leftovers (leftovers?) in a covered container in the refrigerator. The Gooey Fudge Sauce may be refrigerated for up to 3 days. Reheat in a saucepan over very low heat, stirring frequently, or in the microwave on medium power.

For the Gooey Fudge Sauce: In a medium saucepan, combine the cream, butter, brown sugar, granulated sugar, and salt and bring to a simmer over medium heat, stirring to dissolve the sugar. Once sugar is dissolved, reduce heat to medium-low and simmer, stirring occasionally, for 2 minutes. Whisk in the cocoa powder until smooth.

Remove from heat and transfer the sauce to a bowl and stir in the vanilla. Serve hot or warm. Yield: 1 cup.

For the Smooth and Silky Fudge Sauce: In a 3 quart saucepan, combine the chocolate, butter, sugar, and half-and-half, mixing well. Cook, stirring constantly, over medium heat until mixture boils.

Reduce heat to low and cook 5 minutes, stirring constantly. Remove saucepan from heat and stir in the vanilla. Yield: 2 cups.

From Bev and John Shaffer, *No Reservations Required* (Wooster, OH: Wooster Book Company, 2003). Reprinted by permission of the publisher.

For Bev's Hot Fudge Sauce: In a medium saucepan, bring the cream, corn syrup, sugar, cocoa powder, salt, and chocolate to a boil over medium heat, stirring until chocolate is melted.

Reduce heat and simmer, stirring frequently, until some of the liquid has evaporated and mixture has thickened. Remove saucepan from heat and stir in vanilla until blended. Cool sauce to warm and serve. Yield: ⅔ cup.

Chocolate Cupcakes with Chocolate Fudge Frosting

Deliciously decadent fudge frosting tops these cupcakes. Skip the cupcake shop and make your own today!

CUPCAKES

4 tbsp. unsalted butter
¼ cup light olive oil
½ cup water
1 cup unbleached, all-purpose flour
1 cup granulated sugar
¼ cup plus 2 tbsp. unsweetened cocoa powder (not Dutch process), sifted
¾ tsp. baking soda
⅛ tsp. salt
1 large egg
¼ cup buttermilk
1 tsp. vanilla extract

FROSTING

12 oz. bittersweet chocolate, coarsely chopped
1 cup unsalted butter, cut into pieces
⅔ cup milk, whole or 2%
1 tsp. vanilla extract
3¼ cups confectioners' sugar, sifted

For the Cupcakes: Heat oven to 350 degrees. Line a 12-cup cupcake pan with paper liners.

In a medium saucepan, melt the butter with the oil and water over low heat.

In a large bowl, whisk together the flour, sugar, cocoa powder, baking soda, and salt. Add the melted butter mixture, beating with a handheld mixer on low speed until smooth.

Add the egg, beating until blended, then add the buttermilk and vanilla and beat until smooth, stopping to scrape the sides of the bowl.

Scoop the batter into the lined pan, filling each liner about ¾ full. Bake for 25 minutes until springy and a toothpick inserted in the center comes out clean. Let the cupcakes cool slightly in the pan before transferring them to a wire rack to cool completely. Yield: 12 cupcakes.

For the Fudge Frosting: In a medium saucepan, melt the chocolate and butter over low heat, stirring often, until melted and smooth. Remove from heat and cool slightly.

In a large bowl, whisk together the milk, vanilla, and confectioners' sugar until smooth. Add the cooled chocolate mixture and stir until smooth.

Allow the frosting to set and thicken slightly before using. Yield: about 2½ cups, enough for 1 batch of cupcakes.

Cupcakes so moist and fudgy—who can wait to get them out of their papers?

Crispy Chocolate Snaps

Make smaller-sized versions of these chocolate delights for your holiday cookie trays, and keep the large ones at home for yourself!

- 2 cups granulated sugar, plus extra for rolling dough
- 1 cup light brown sugar, firmly packed
- 1½ cups unsalted butter, room temperature
- 2 tsp. vanilla extract
- 3 large eggs
- 6 oz. unsweetened chocolate, melted and cooled
- 4 cups unbleached, all-purpose flour
- 2 tsp. baking soda
- 1 tsp. salt

Bev's Bites

If you have a tendency to peek through the oven window while cookies bake, don't get nervous—these cookies puff up then flatten during baking.

In the large bowl of an electric mixer, beat granulated sugar and brown sugar with butter until light and fluffy. Scrape down the sides of the bowl.

Beat in vanilla, eggs, and unsweetened chocolate, blending well. Stir in flour, baking soda, and salt and beat until combined.

Cover and refrigerate dough for 6 to 24 hours to allow flavors to meld and dough to be easier to handle.

Heat oven to 350 degrees. Line cookie sheets with parchment paper or silicone liners.

Shape dough into 1½" balls and roll in granulated sugar. Place 3" apart on prepared cookie sheets. Bake for 8 to 12 minutes or until set.

Cool 1 minute, then remove from cookie sheets and allow to cool completely on wire racks. Yield: 6 dozen cookies.

Individual Hot Chocolate Cakes

Fun little comfort cakes . . . no sharing allowed!

1¾ cups unbleached, all-purpose flour
2 cups granulated sugar
½ cup unsweetened cocoa powder (preferably Dutch process), plus additional for dusting cakes
¼ cup your favorite hot chocolate mix
2 tsp. baking soda
1 tsp. baking powder
1 tsp. salt
1 cup buttermilk
2 large eggs
1¼ tsp. vanilla extract
½ cup light olive oil
1 cup strong brewed coffee, room temperature
2 cups heavy whipping cream, whipped, for serving

Heat oven to 300 degrees.

In a medium bowl, whisk together the flour, sugar, cocoa powder, hot chocolate mix, baking soda, baking powder, and salt.

In a large bowl, whisk together the buttermilk, eggs, vanilla, oil, and coffee. Slowly add the dry ingredients into the wet, ⅓ at a time, whisking in between each addition to blend.

Arrange 8 8-oz. Mason (canning) jars on a baking sheet and carefully pour ½ cup of the batter into each jar. Place the baking sheet in the oven and bake the cakes until a toothpick inserted in the center comes out clean, about 35 to 40 minutes.

Remove from the oven and allow to cool slightly on a wire rack. Serve warm, topping each cake with whipped cream and a dusting of cocoa powder. (Use caution, as the jars might still be hot.) Yield: 8 individual cakes.

Rustic baking gets sophisticated with these flavorful, individual chocolate cakes baked in Mason jars and dolloped with whipped cream.

Comfort Chocolate

Simply Sublime Double-Chocolate Pudding

Pudding from scratch is so easy and so sublime! Give away that boxed mix once and for all.

¾ cup granulated sugar
⅓ cup unsweetened cocoa powder, sifted
3 tbsp. cornstarch
¼ tsp. salt
2 cups half-and-half, divided
3 oz. bittersweet chocolate, coarsely chopped
1½ tsp. vanilla extract

In a medium saucepan, whisk together the sugar, cocoa powder, cornstarch, and salt. Gradually whisk in 1 cup of the half-and-half until mixture is smooth. Whisk in the remaining 1 cup of half-and-half.

Cook over medium heat, whisking constantly, until the mixture thickens and comes to a boil. Continue to whisk and boil for 1 minute.

Remove the pan from the heat. Add the chocolate and vanilla. Let stand for about 6 minutes or until the chocolate is melted, then stir gently until the pudding is smooth.

Divide among 4 dessert dishes. Place a piece of plastic wrap or wax paper directly on top of each pudding to prevent a "skin" from forming. Allow to cool for 15 minutes and serve warm and soft. Alternately, chill for at least up to 8 hours and serve cold. Yield: 4 servings.

White Chocolate Bread Pudding with White Chocolate Sauce

Served with tart, fresh, seasonal berries, this white chocolate combo is rich and satisfyingly sweet.

BREAD PUDDING

8 oz. French bread, cut into 1" pieces
3 cups heavy cream
1 cup milk, 2%
½ cup granulated sugar
10 oz. white chocolate, coarsely chopped
7 large egg yolks
2 large eggs

WHITE CHOCOLATE SAUCE

½ cup heavy whipping cream
8 oz. white chocolate, coarsely chopped

Bev's Bites

May be prepared 1 day ahead up through baking. Cover with foil and refrigerate; to rewarm, place covered pudding in a 350-degree oven for 30 minutes before serving.

For the Bread Pudding: Heat oven to 300 degrees.

Arrange bread cubes on a baking sheet and bake until light golden and dry, about 10 minutes. Transfer baking sheet to a wire rack and cool completely. Increase oven temperature to 350 degrees.

In a large saucepan, combine the heavy cream, milk, and sugar and bring to a simmer over medium heat, stirring until sugar dissolves. Remove saucepan from heat.

Add white chocolate and stir until melted and smooth.

In a large bowl, whisk the yolks and eggs to blend. Gradually whisk in the warm chocolate mixture.

Place bread cubes in a 3-quart baking dish. Add half of the chocolate-egg mixture. Press bread cubes into mixture and let stand 15 minutes. Gently mix in remaining chocolate mixture and cover dish with foil.

Bake for 45 minutes, then uncover and bake until top is golden brown, about 15 minutes. Transfer pudding to rack and cool slightly.

For the White Chocolate Sauce: Bring the heavy cream to a simmer. Remove saucepan from the heat and stir in white chocolate until smooth.

Top warm Bread Pudding with warm White Chocolate Sauce. Yield: 6 servings.

Comfort Chocolate

Buttermilk Chocolate Bread with Chocolate Honey Butter

My favorite fudge sauce to use in the Chocolate Honey Butter is my Smooth and Silky Fudge Sauce, but any of the fudge sauces in this book would make a great ingredient.

BREAD

- 1 cup granulated sugar
- ½ cup unsalted butter, room temperature, cut into pieces
- 2 large eggs
- 1 cup buttermilk
- 1¾ cups unbleached, all-purpose flour
- ½ cup unsweetened cocoa powder, sifted
- ½ tsp. baking powder
- ½ tsp. baking soda
- ½ tsp. salt
- ⅓ cup chopped walnuts, optional

CHOCOLATE HONEY BUTTER

- ½ cup unsalted butter, room temperature, cut into pieces
- 2 tbsp. honey
- 2 tbsp. fudge sauce, room temperature

Bev's Bites

No buttermilk in the refrigerator? Use 1 tbsp. of vinegar or lemon juice plus milk to make 1 cup. Allow to sit for 15 minutes before using.

For the Bread: Heat oven to 350 degrees. Grease only the bottom of an 8½" x 4½" or 9" x 5" loaf pan.

In the large bowl of an electric mixer, beat the sugar and butter until light and fluffy. Beat in the eggs, one at a time, until blended.

Stir in the buttermilk, then add the flour, cocoa powder, baking powder, baking soda, and salt, mixing just until dry particles are moistened. Quickly stir in nuts, if using. Do not over mix, or the bread texture will be tough.

Pour batter into prepared pan. Bake for 55 to 60 minutes or until a toothpick inserted in the center comes out clean. Cool in pan on wire rack for 30 minutes, then remove bread from pan and cool completely on a wire rack before slicing. Yield: 12 servings.

For the Honey Butter: In the small bowl of an electric mixer, combine the butter, honey, and fudge sauce. Beat at medium-high speed until light and fluffy. Yield: 1 cup.

Enjoy a spot of afternoon tea served with Buttermilk Chocolate Bread with Chocolate Honey Butter.

Bev's Bittersweet Chocolate Waffles

A spectacular dessert. I like to serve it with chocolate chip ice cream and one of my fudge sauces. For those less daring, dust with confectioners' sugar and serve with fresh strawberries and raspberries.

- 1 cup unbleached, all-purpose flour
- ¼ cup unsweetened cocoa powder, sifted
- 1¼ tsp. baking powder
- ¼ tsp. baking soda
- ⅛ tsp. salt
- ¼ cup granulated sugar
- 3 oz. semisweet chocolate, finely chopped
- 4 tbsp. unsalted butter
- 2 large eggs
- 1 cup plus 3 tbsp. milk, whole or 2%
- 1 tsp. vanilla extract
- Fudge sauce, chocolate chip ice cream, confectioners' sugar, fresh berries, or any other desired topping

In a large bowl, sift together the flour, cocoa powder, baking powder, baking soda, and salt. Mix in the sugar.

In a small saucepan, melt the chocolate and butter, whisking until smooth. Pour mixture into a medium bowl and allow to cool slightly. Whisk in the eggs, milk, and vanilla.

Make a well (hole) in the center of the dry ingredients and gradually whisk in the milk mixture.

Heat your waffle maker, then make waffles with the batter. Place on a serving plate and top as desired. Yield: will depend on your waffle maker, but generally 4 to 6 servings.

Not-Just-for-Tree-Huggin'-Hippies Chocolate Granola

Delicious by itself, with yogurt or fresh berries, or as a frozen yogurt parfait. Peace, love, and chocolate granola—what else do you need?

6 cups old-fashioned rolled oats
½ cup flax seeds
1 cup pecans, coarsely chopped
½ cup roasted and lightly salted, blanched peanuts
⅓ cup extra-light olive oil or canola oil
⅔ cup honey
2 tsp. vanilla extract
6 oz. bittersweet chocolate, coarsely chopped
1¼ cups dried tart cherries or cranberries, coarsely chopped

Heat oven to 300 degrees.

In a large bowl, combine the oats, flax seeds, pecans, and peanuts.

In a small saucepan, warm the oil and honey; whisk in the vanilla to combine. Pour over oat mixture and mix well.

Spread mixture into a large jellyroll pan or two 13" x 9" baking pans. Bake for 15 minutes, then stir well. Bake for an additional 10 minutes, then stir well. Bake for an additional 5 minutes or until a light golden brown.

Remove from oven and sprinkle chopped chocolate over mixture while it is still hot, stirring the baked mixture to thoroughly combine chocolate. Mix in dried cherries or cranberries. Cool completely. Yield: 10 cups.

Not-Just-for-Tree-Huggin'-Hippies Chocolate Granola and yogurt parfaits—groovy, man!

Hot Chocolate: Comfort in a Cup
Try them all and pick your fave!

CLASSIC HOT COCOA

⅓ cup unsweetened cocoa powder, sifted
3 to 4 tbsp. granulated sugar
Pinch of salt
2½ cups milk, whole, divided
Mini marshmallows, for garnish

Bev's Bites
For best flavor, do not let the cocoa boil.

RICH AND CHOCOLATY HOT CHOCOLATE

2 tbsp. granulated sugar
4 tsp. unsweetened cocoa powder, sifted
1 cup milk, low-fat, divided
¼ tsp. vanilla extract
Pinch of ground cinnamon

Bev's Bites
To froth the hot chocolate, whirl a whisk in the saucepan by rubbing your hands back and forth.

FROZEN HOT CHOCOLATE

2½ cups plus 2 tbsp. milk, whole
½ cup unsweetened cocoa powder
¾ cup granulated sugar

For the Classic Hot Cocoa: In a medium saucepan, combine the cocoa powder, sugar, and salt. Whisk in ¼ cup of the milk, whisking constantly until the mixture is smooth and free of lumps.

Whisk in the remaining 1¼ cups milk to combine. Set the saucepan over medium to medium-high heat and whisk frequently until hot.

Serve hot, topped with mini marshmallows. Yield: 2 servings.

For the Rich and Chocolaty Hot Chocolate: Mix the sugar, cocoa powder, and 2 tbsp. of the milk in a mug until smooth.

In a small saucepan, heat the remaining milk until steaming hot but not boiling. Stir in the cocoa mixture and add the vanilla.

Pour the hot mixture back into the mug and sprinkle with cinnamon. Yield: 1 serving.

For the Frozen Hot Chocolate: In a medium saucepan, combine 2½ cups of the milk, cocoa powder, and sugar and bring to a simmer over medium heat, whisking until cocoa and sugar are dissolved.

Transfer to a bowl and chill, covered, for 2 hours. Pour mixture into a 13" x 9" baking pan and freeze until solid, about 8 hours.

Let frozen mixture stand at room temperature just until easy enough to break into small pieces, about 3 to 5 minutes. Transfer pieces to a blender. Add remaining milk and blend just until mixture is slushy. Serve immediately. Yield: 4 servings.

BED AND BREAKFAST HOT CHOCOLATE

8 oz. semisweet chocolate, finely chopped
½ cup water
¼ cup light corn syrup
¼ cup granulated sugar
2 tbsp. unsalted butter, room temperature
6 cups milk or half-and-half

Bev's Bites

Once the butter is blended, the mixture may be refrigerated up to one month.

For a single 10-oz. serving, use 2 heaping tbsp. of the chocolate base.

PARISIAN HOT CHOCOLATE

2 cups milk
¾ cup heavy whipping cream, divided
¼ cup unsweetened cocoa powder, preferably Dutch process
6 oz. bittersweet or semisweet chocolate, very finely chopped
1 tsp. vanilla extract
1 tsp. superfine sugar

VENEZUELAN HOT COCOA

2 cups milk, whole
¼ tsp. ground cinnamon
2"-long strip orange peel
3½ oz. bittersweet chocolate, coarsely chopped

For the Bed and Breakfast Hot Chocolate: Place chopped chocolate in a medium bowl and set aside.

In a small saucepan over medium heat, combine water, corn syrup, and sugar. Bring barely to a boil, then immediately pour over the chocolate. Whisk until chocolate is melted and completely smooth. Whisk in butter until blended.

In a medium saucepan, combine chocolate mixture and milk, whisking constantly until very hot but not boiling. Serve immediately. Yield: 4 servings.

For the Parisian Hot Chocolate: In a medium saucepan, combine the milk, ½ cup of the cream, and cocoa powder. Warm over medium heat, stirring to dissolve the cocoa.

Add the chopped chocolate and stir until completely melted, then reduce heat to low and bring mixture to a simmer. (Do not boil.) Return the heat to medium and cook for 5 minutes, stirring occasionally. Remove mixture from heat and stir in vanilla. Let cool briefly before ladling into serving cups.

Whip the remaining ¼ cup cream with the superfine sugar until soft peaks form. Place a dollop of the whipped cream on each serving of hot chocolate. Yield: 4 servings.

For the Venezuelan Hot Cocoa: In a small saucepan, bring the milk, cinnamon, and orange peel to a simmer, whisking briefly to blend the cinnamon.

Remove from heat, cover, and let stand 5 minutes. Discard orange peel.

Add chocolate to saucepan, cover, and let stand 1 additional minute or until chocolate has melted, then whisk until smooth.

Reheat mixture and pour into mugs. Yield: 2 servings.

Comfort Chocolate

Chocolate Crumb-Crusted Chocolate-Caramel Cheesecake

Intensely dark chocolate with a creamy caramel flavor...

CHOCOLATE CRUMB CRUST

1½ cups (5 oz.) chocolate wafers, finely ground
5 tbsp. unsalted butter, melted
⅓ cup granulated sugar
⅛ tsp. salt

CHEESECAKE

1 cup granulated sugar
¾ cup heavy whipping cream
8 oz. bittersweet chocolate, coarsely chopped
½ cup sour cream, room temperature
24 oz. cream cheese, room temperature, cut into pieces
4 large eggs
1 tsp. vanilla extract

For the Crust: Stir together the wafer crumbs, butter, sugar, and salt and press onto the bottom and ½" to 1" up the sides of a lightly greased 9½" or 10" springform pan. Chill until ready to fill.

For the Cheesecake: Heat oven to 350 degrees.

In a medium saucepan, heat sugar over medium-low heat, stirring slowly with a fork, until melted and pale golden. Cook without stirring, swirling pan occasionally, until a deep golden color. Remove from heat and carefully add heavy cream (the mixture will vigorously steam and harden).

Return pan to medium-low heat, stirring, until caramel is dissolved. Remove saucepan from heat and whisk in chocolate until smooth. Stir in sour cream.

In the large bowl of an electric mixer, beat cream cheese until fluffy. Scrape down the sides of the bowl, then beat in the chocolate-caramel mixture on low speed. Beat in eggs, one at a time, scraping down the sides of the bowl between each addition. Add vanilla and beat until incorporated.

Place the prepared springform pan on a shallow baking sheet to catch any drips. Pour filling into crust and bake in the middle of the oven for 60 minutes, or until cake is set 3" from the edge but center is still slightly wobbly when gently shaken. The cheesecake will continue to set as it cools.

Remove from oven and run a knife between the cake and the pan to loosen. Cool completely in the springform pan on a wire rack. Chill, loosely covered, at least 6 hours.

Transfer cheesecake to a plate. Bring to room temperature before serving. Yield: 8 to 10 servings.

Hints of caramel add an extra layer of flavor to this creamy, dreamy chocolate cheesecake.

Gluten-Free Swirled Brownie Cheesecake Squares

Treat those gluten-free friends with these moist, swirly brownie squares.

Unsweetened cocoa powder, sifted, for dusting pan

CHEESECAKE BASE

- 12 oz. cream cheese, room temperature
- ¼ cup granulated sugar
- 1½ tsp. gluten-free vanilla
- 2 large eggs, lightly beaten
- ¼ cup heavy whipping cream

BROWNIE BASE

- 1 cup unsalted butter, room temperature
- 8 oz. unsweetened baking chocolate, coarsely chopped
- 3 cups granulated sugar
- 4 large eggs
- ½ cup milk, whole or 2%
- 2 tsp. gluten-free vanilla
- 2 cups gluten-free all-purpose flour mix
- ½ tsp. salt

Heat oven to 325 degrees. Lightly grease and dust with cocoa powder a nonstick 13" x 9" baking pan.

For the Cheesecake Base: In the medium bowl of an electric mixer, beat the cream cheese, sugar, and vanilla until light and smooth. Add eggs, one at a time, beating well after each addition. Beat in cream. Set aside.

For the Brownie Base: In a large saucepan, melt the butter and chocolate over low heat, stirring until smooth. Remove from heat and allow mixture to cool to lukewarm.

Add the sugar to chocolate, whisking to combine. Stir in the eggs, one at a time, mixing well after each addition. Stir in the milk and vanilla.

In a small bowl, whisk together the flour mix and salt. Stir into the chocolate mixture just until blended.

Spread *half* of the brownie base into prepared pan. Drop tablespoonfuls of *half* of the cheesecake base on top of the brownie base.

Lightly and gently spread the remaining brownie base over the top. Drop tablespoonfuls of the remaining cheesecake base on top of that, then lightly and gently swirl both mixtures together.

Bake for 25 to 35 minutes or until center is almost set. Remove from oven and cool on a wire rack.

Refrigerate for at least 4 hours or overnight. When ready to serve, cut into squares. Yield: 2 to 3 dozen pieces.

Rich, Chocolaty Crème Fraîche Cupcakes

Wonderfully rich and heavenly, topped with tangy crème fraîche—what a treat!

- 1 cup plus 3 tbsp. unbleached, all-purpose flour
- ⅔ cup unsweetened cocoa powder
- 1 tsp. baking powder
- ¼ tsp. baking soda
- 1 tsp. salt
- ½ cup plus 6 tbsp. unsalted butter, room temperature, cut into pieces
- 1 cup granulated sugar
- 3 large eggs
- 1 tsp. vanilla extract
- ¾ cup crème fraîche, room temperature, well stirred, plus additional for topping cupcakes

Heat oven to 350 degrees. Line a 12-cup cupcake pan with foil baking cups. Line four additional cups in another pan for "overflow" batter.

In a medium bowl, sift together the flour, cocoa powder, baking powder, baking soda, and salt. Set aside.

In the large bowl of an electric mixer, beat the butter and sugar until light and fluffy. Scrape down the sides of the bowl. At medium speed, add the eggs, one at a time, beating until each one is fully incorporated before adding the next. Stir in vanilla.

At low speed, alternate beating the dry ingredients and the crème fraîche into the butter-egg mixture in two batches.

Spoon the batter into the foil cups, filling each ⅔ full. Bake for 15 to 20 minutes or until springy when gently pressed and a cake tester or toothpick inserted in the center comes out clean. Let cool slightly before removing from pan.

Place a dollop of crème fraîche on each cupcake and serve. Yield: 16 cupcakes.

Fudge Pudding Cake
No garnish is necessary for this fudgy wonder.

1¼ cups unbleached, all-purpose flour
1¾ cups granulated sugar, divided
¼ cup unsweetened cocoa powder, sifted, divided
1½ tsp. baking powder
½ tsp. salt
½ cup milk, whole or 2%
2 tbsp. unsalted butter, melted
1 tsp. vanilla extract
1⅓ cups hot water

Heat oven to 350 degrees.

In a medium bowl, combine the flour, ¾ cup sugar, 2 tbsp. of the cocoa powder, baking powder, and salt.

Stir in the milk, butter, and vanilla until well blended; spread into a 9" round or square baking pan.

In a small bowl, combine the remaining 1 cup sugar and 2 tbsp. cocoa powder. Sprinkle mixture evenly over the cake batter. Carefully pour hot water over sugar mixture.

Bake for 35 to 45 minutes or until center is set and firm to the touch. Serve warm. Yield: 8 servings.

Chocolate Casserole
A truly rich, decadent conversation starter.

½ cup unbleached, all-purpose flour
¾ cup granulated sugar, divided
¾ tsp. baking powder
⅓ cup milk, whole or 2%
1 tbsp. canola oil
1 tsp. vanilla extract
¼ cup peanut butter
⅓ cup semisweet chocolate, coarsely chopped
¼ cup unsweetened cocoa powder, sifted
¾ cup boiling water
⅓ cup coarsely chopped honey-roasted peanuts
2 tbsp. crumbled chocolate-flavored graham crackers
Whipped cream, for serving (oh come on, why not?)

Heat oven to 350 degrees.

In a medium bowl, combine the flour, ¼ cup of the sugar, and baking powder. Whisk in milk, oil, and vanilla until smooth.

Stir in peanut butter and chocolate pieces. Pour batter into an ungreased 1½-quart casserole dish. Set aside.

In small bowl, stir together the remaining ½ cup of sugar and cocoa powder. Gradually whisk in boiling water, then pour mixture evenly over batter in casserole dish.

Bake uncovered for 35 to 40 minutes or until a wooden toothpick inserted into the "cake" portion comes out clean. Remove from the oven and top with peanuts and graham cracker pieces.

Serve warm with whipped cream. Yield: 6 to 8 servings.

Warm Chocolate Beignets

A chocolate version of a New Orleans classic—warm, they'd make Café du Monde proud.

2½ tsp. (1 packet) active dry yeast
5 oz. warm water, 105 to 115 degrees
3 oz. warm milk, whole or 2%
2 oz. unsalted butter, melted
2 large eggs, beaten
2¾ cups unbleached, all-purpose flour
1 cup unsweetened cocoa powder, sifted
½ cup plus 3 tbsp. granulated sugar
1 tsp. salt
12 oz. white chocolate, coarsely chopped
Vegetable oil, for frying
Confectioners' sugar, for dusting

Dissolve yeast in water. Stir in milk, butter, and eggs.

In a large bowl, combine the flour, cocoa powder, sugar, and salt. Add the yeast mixture and stir to form a dough.

Place dough in a lightly oiled bowl; wrap and refrigerate overnight to allow dough to slowly rise and double in size.

Knead dough for 3 to 5 minutes until elastic, then roll into a rectangle about ¼" thick. Cut dough into 2" squares.

In the center of half of the squares, place a portion of the white chocolate. Top with the remaining squares, pressing edges together to seal well. Let rise, lightly covered, for 1½ hours.

Heat oil to 350 degrees and fry beignets, a few at a time, for 45 seconds or just until crisped.

Drain well on a rack on top of paper towels. Dust generously with confectioners' sugar and serve immediately. Yield: 20 beignets.

Chocolate Chocolate Chipotle Fudge Milkshake

When just one type of chocolate won't do . . . and you need a kick to go with it.

1 cup chocolate milk
1 pint chocolate ice cream
1 to 1½ tsp. chipotle chili powder (depending on how spicy hot you'd like it!)
4 tbsp. fudge sauce

Bev's Bites

I prefer using a Vitamix blender, but if you don't have access to one, try blending on the High setting of your own blender.

Place the milk, ice cream, chili powder, and fudge sauce into the container of a Vitamix blender.

Secure lid and select Variable 1, then slowly increase speed to Variable 10, then High. Blend just until well combined, using the tamper only if needed.

Serve immediately. Yield: 2 servings.

Set your chocolate meter on high and slowly sip and indulge in this Chocolate Chocolate Chipotle Fudge Milkshake—easily made in my favorite (Vitamix) blender.

Loaded Chocolate-Pecan Coffee Cake

Crumbly in a good way, this cake is easy to assemble and even easier to eat.

- ½ cup unsalted butter, room temperature
- 1 cup granulated sugar
- 2 large eggs
- 1 tsp. vanilla
- 1 cup plain Greek yogurt, well drained
- 2 cups unbleached, all-purpose flour
- 1½ tsp. baking powder
- 1 tsp. baking soda
- ¼ tsp. salt
- 1 cup (about 5 oz.) semisweet chocolate, coarsely chopped
- 1 tbsp. ground cinnamon
- 1 cup toasted, salted pecans, coarsely chopped
- ½ cup light brown sugar, firmly packed
- Grated chocolate, for serving

Heat oven to 350 degrees. Lightly grease and flour a 9" square baking pan.

In the large bowl of an electric mixer, cream butter and granulated sugar until light and fluffy. Beat in eggs and vanilla; stop and scrape down the sides of the bowl. Blend in yogurt.

In a large bowl, whisk together the flour, baking powder, baking soda, and salt. Blend into the yogurt mixture, mixing well.

Spread *half* the batter into the pan. Batter will be thin.

In a medium bowl, mix together the chocolate, cinnamon, pecans, and brown sugar. Sprinkle *half* of this mixture over batter in pan.

Spoon remaining batter evenly over the chocolate-nut mixture; gently spread as best you can to create an even top.

Sprinkle remaining chocolate-nut mixture over the top. Bake 35 to 45 minutes or until a toothpick inserted in the middle comes out clean. Cool in pan 10 to 15 minutes before serving. Serve warm, topped with additional grated chocolate, if desired. Yield: 12 servings.

Crumbly, nutty, and chocolatey— it's snack time, anytime!

A crisp, buttery shortbread cookie with an intensely dark chocolate filling. What's not to like?

The Bitter and the (Mostly) Sweet Thumbprint Cookies

Eating just one takes so much willpower.

COOKIES

2 cups unbleached, all-purpose flour
½ tsp. baking powder
¼ tsp. salt
½ cup plus 6 tbsp. unsalted butter, room temperature
¾ cup granulated sugar
1 large egg
1¼ tsp. vanilla extract

CHOCOLATE CREAM FILLING

6 oz. bittersweet or semisweet chocolate, finely chopped
¼ cup plus 2 tbsp. heavy whipping cream

For the Cookies: Heat oven to 350 degrees.

In a medium bowl, whisk together the flour, baking powder, and salt. Set aside.

In the large bowl of an electric mixer, beat the butter and sugar on medium speed until light and fluffy. Scrape down the sides of the bowl. Beat in the egg and vanilla. With the mixer on low speed, beat in the flour mixture in two batches.

Roll slightly rounded teaspoons of the dough into 1" balls and place them 1½" apart on ungreased baking sheets. With your thumb, make a deep indentation in the center of each ball.

Bake for 10 to 14 minutes, rotating the baking sheets 180 degrees halfway through baking (around 5 to 7 minutes in), until cookies are a light golden brown. Cool on baking sheets for 2 minutes, then transfer the cookies to wire racks to cool completely.

For the Filling: Place the chocolate in a medium bowl.

In a small saucepan, bring the cream to a boil and pour the hot cream over the chocolate. Let stand for 1 minute, then whisk gently until the chocolate is melted and smooth.

Let cool, stirring occasionally, until the mixture is thick enough to hold its shape when dropped from a spoon but not yet set, about 45 minutes to 1 hour.

Spoon the filling into a pastry bag or a small resealable plastic bag. If using a plastic baggie, snip off a small piece of the tip of one of the bottom corners. Pipe a dollop of filling into the center of each cookie. Let the cookies rest until the filling has set, unless of course you need to test one to make sure that they are okay to share. Yield: 2½ dozen cookies.

Chocolate Chocolate Cocoa Cookies
Chocolate goodness abounds in these signature cookies.

4 oz. unsweetened chocolate, coarsely chopped
6 oz. semisweet chocolate, coarsely chopped
½ cup unsalted butter, room temperature
4 large eggs, lightly beaten
1 cup granulated sugar
½ cup light brown sugar, firmly packed
1½ tbsp. unsweetened cocoa powder, sifted
2 tsp. vanilla extract
½ cup unbleached, all-purpose flour
¼ tsp. salt
½ tsp. baking powder
2 oz. bittersweet chocolate, coarsely chopped

Bev's Bites
Chilling the dough creates a puffier cookie.

Heat oven to 350 degrees. Line two or three cookies sheets with parchment paper or silicone liners.

Melt the unsweetened and semisweet chocolates together, then whisk in the butter to blend. Set aside.

In the large bowl of an electric mixer, beat eggs, granulated sugar, and brown sugar on medium-high speed until mixture is thick and well blended. Beat in cocoa powder and vanilla. Scrape down the sides of the bowl.

Stir in flour, salt, and baking powder. On low speed, gently blend in melted chocolate mixture. Scrape down the sides of the bowl. Stir in chocolate pieces.

Cover batter and chill for 1 to 24 hours.

Drop by heaping tablespoonful onto prepared cookie sheets, keeping in mind that batter will spread during baking. Bake for 9 to 10 minutes until cookies are puffy.

Cool completely on a wire rack. Yield: 3½ to 4 dozen.

From Bev Shaffer, *Brownies to Die For!* (Gretna, LA: Pelican, 2006). Reprinted by permission of the publisher.

Intense flavors make this crisp cookie the perfect chocolate pick-me-up!

*Layers of sweet buttery nuts and a fudgy chocolate filling . . .
a flavor extravaganza in every dreamy bite.*

Fudge Nut Deep-Dish Pie

Pecans or pistachios make for an interesting substitute for walnuts in this recipe.

NUT CRUST

- 3 cups walnut pieces, lightly toasted
- 4 tsp. granulated sugar
- 5 tbsp. unsalted butter, room temperature, cut into small pieces

FUDGE FILLING

- 12 oz. bittersweet chocolate, coarsely chopped
- ½ cup plus 2 tbsp. unsalted butter, room temperature, cut into pieces
- 1½ tsp. vanilla extract
- 5 large egg yolks
- 4 large eggs
- ½ cup superfine sugar

FUDGE GLAZE

- 2 oz. bittersweet chocolate, coarsely chopped
- 1 tbsp. heavy whipping cream or whole milk
- ½ tsp. hot water
- ½ tsp. light corn syrup
- ¼ tsp. vanilla extract

Heat oven to 325 degrees.

For the Crust: Butter and flour a deep-dish 9½" pie plate. Set aside.

Pulse the walnuts and sugar in a food processor until walnuts are chopped into medium-sized pieces. Empty mixture into a bowl and work in softened butter with your fingertips. Measure 1 cup of mixture and sprinkle it evenly onto the bottom of prepared pie plate.

Place a piece of waxed paper over mixture and use the bottom of a flat glass to press nuts firmly and evenly into the pie plate to form a nut layer covering just the bottom.

For the Filling: Melt chocolate. Blend in butter, one tablespoon at a time, mashing it as needed. Add vanilla.

In the large bowl of an electric mixer with the whisk attachment, beat egg yolks and eggs on medium-high speed until thickened and light in color, about 4 minutes. Add the superfine sugar, one tablespoon at a time, until blended. Reduce speed to low and blend in the melted chocolate mixture.

Pour half of the filling into the nut-lined pie plate. Sprinkle with half of the remaining nut mixture. Top with remaining filling, then scatter remaining nut mixture over the top.

Bake for 40 to 45 minutes or until a toothpick inserted into center is slightly moist, but not wet. Do not over bake or pie filling will be dry.

Allow to cool and set for 6 to 8 hours. As the pie cools, the center will firm up.

For the Glaze: Place the chocolate, cream, water, corn syrup, and vanilla in a glass bowl set on top of a pan of simmering water. Stir frequently until chocolate is melted and mixture is smooth.

Cool slightly, then drizzle glaze over top of cooled pie using a fork or small spoon. Yield: 8 to 10 servings.

Cocoa-Buttermilk Cake with Cocoa-Mascarpone Frosting

This recipe is sure to become a favorite . . . it's rich and dense and delicious, and it freezes well, too!

COCOA-BUTTERMILK CAKE

2⅓ cups unbleached, all-purpose flour
¾ cup unsweetened Dutch process cocoa powder or unsweetened cocoa powder, sifted
1 tsp. baking soda
¾ tsp. baking powder
½ tsp. salt
¾ cup unsalted butter, room temperature
1 cup granulated sugar
1 cup light brown sugar, firmly packed
3 large eggs, room temperature
2 tsp. vanilla
1½ cups buttermilk

COCOA-MASCARPONE FROSTING

4 oz. mascarpone, room temperature
½ cup unsalted butter, room temperature
⅓ cup Dutch process unsweetened cocoa powder or unsweetened cocoa powder, sifted
2 to 4 tbsp. milk, divided, plus additional as needed
2 tsp. vanilla
4¼ cups confectioners' sugar, sifted

For the Cake: Lightly grease a 13" x 9" baking pan. Heat oven to 350 degrees.

In a medium bowl, whisk together the flour, cocoa powder, baking soda, baking powder, and salt. Set aside.

In the large bowl of an electric mixer, beat butter on medium-high speed for 30 seconds. Stop and scrape down the sides of the bowl and the beater.

Gradually add granulated sugar and brown sugar to butter, beating on medium speed until combined. Stop and scrape down the sides of the bowl; beat for 2 additional minutes.

Add eggs, one at a time, beating well after each addition. Beat in vanilla.

Alternate adding the flour mixture with the buttermilk, beating on low speed after each addition just until combined. Beat on medium-high speed for 20 seconds more until well blended. Pour batter into the prepared pan, spreading evenly.

Bake for 25 to 35 minutes or until a wooden toothpick inserted in the center comes out clean. Cool cake completely on a wire rack. Yield: 12 to 16 servings.

For the Frosting: In the large bowl of an electric mixer, beat the mascarpone, butter, cocoa powder, 2 tbsp. of the milk, and vanilla on medium to high speed until creamy.

Gradually add the confectioners' sugar, beating until smooth, stopping often to scrape down the sides of the bowl and beater.

Beat in enough additional milk (1 tablespoon at a time), as needed, to reach spreading consistency. Yield: 2½ cups.

Frost cake with Cocoa-Mascarpone Frosting. Cake may be stored, lightly covered, in the refrigerator.

Everything an easy chocolate cake should be—rich and moist with an extra helping of can't-get-enough chocolate flavor.

Mocha Cupcakes with White Chocolate Cream Cheese Drizzle

Just a little drizzle does the trick, enough for each perfect bite and lick.

CUPCAKES

2⅔ cups unbleached, all-purpose flour
1½ cups unsweetened cocoa powder, sifted
1 tbsp. ground cinnamon
1½ tsp. baking powder
1½ tsp. salt
1 tsp. baking soda
3½ cups granulated sugar
1¼ cups brewed coffee, room temperature
1¼ cups buttermilk
¾ cup canola oil or light olive oil
2 large eggs
2 large egg yolks
1 tbsp. vanilla extract
7 oz. semisweet chocolate chips, chopped

DRIZZLE

4½ oz. white chocolate, melted and cooled
6 oz. cream cheese, room temperature, cut into pieces
6 tbsp. unsalted butter, room temperature, cut into pieces
¼ cup confectioners' sugar, sifted
½ tsp. vanilla extract
¼ tsp. salt

For the Cupcakes: Heat oven to 325 degrees. Line 30 cups in cupcake pans with cupcake papers.

In a large bowl, sift together the flour, cocoa powder, cinnamon, baking powder, salt, and baking soda.

In the large bowl of an electric mixer, beat the sugar, coffee, buttermilk, oil, eggs, egg yolks, and vanilla until blended. Scrape down the sides of the bowl. Add the flour mixture and beat on medium speed until blended. Scrape down the sides of the bowl. Stir in chocolate chips.

Spoon ¼ cup of the batter into each cupcake paper. Bake just until firm to the touch, about 20 to 25 minutes. Transfer cupcakes to racks and cool completely.

For the Drizzle: In a medium bowl, beat the cream cheese, butter, confectioners' sugar, vanilla, and salt using a handheld mixer until light and fluffy. Scrape down the sides of the bowl. Gradually beat in the melted white chocolate.

Let cool until thickened to a drizzle consistency. Drizzle over the top of the cupcakes with a fork or a small spoon. Yield: 30 cupcakes.

Baked to perfection, it's time to cool!

If you weren't paying attention, I would have already licked the White Chocolate Cream Cheese Drizzle from the side of this Mocha Cupcake.

CHOCOLATE PAIRINGS

You don't need to be a Double-O agent to treasure every spoonful of these Live and Let Chai Pots de Crème.

What pairs well with chocolate? There are the classics—other chocolates, peanut butter, strawberries, raspberries, vanilla. There are also the bolder flavors of chipotle and hot chilies and the newer chocolate-fruit combos using pineapple and mango. Chocolate accents pork and beef and barbecue sauces.

The perfect chocolate pairings are, well, your imagination and creativity. Explore with me . . .

Chocolate Banana Praline Soufflé

You—yes, you—are more than capable of making light-as-a-feather, buoyant soufflés.

PRALINE

1 cup granulated sugar
¼ cup water
8 oz. pecan pieces, lightly toasted

SOUFFLÉ

4 large egg yolks
2 large ripe bananas, lightly mashed
1 cup grated bittersweet chocolate
1 tbsp. dark rum
6 large egg whites
Pinch of salt
3 tbsp. granulated sugar
½ cup Praline, plus additional for serving
Chocolate ice cream, for serving

Bev's Bites

Tips for soufflé success:
- Use straight-sided soufflé dishes or ramekins. Soufflés will not rise straight and high in a slanted dish.
- To butter the ramekins, first soften the butter to room temperature.
- Use a pastry brush to coat the inside of the soufflé ramekin or dish with the softened butter. Don't forget to include the inside top edge of the dish. This will melt during baking, ensuring that the batter will not stick to the rim of the dish and that the soufflé will rise effortlessly.
- Sprinkle several spoonfuls of sugar into the buttered mold, then tip and shake the mold to distribute the sugar evenly over all surfaces. Tap out any excess. The sugar will provide the soufflé with a sweet, crunchy "crust." (This technique is similar to flouring a greased cake pan.)
- Don't even think about opening the oven during baking! Walk out of the kitchen if you have to. Even the slightest fluctuation in temperature can inhibit proper rising.

For the Praline: Generously butter a baking sheet and set aside.

In a medium saucepan, combine the sugar and water and cook the mixture over medium heat, stirring with a wooden spoon to dissolve the sugar crystals.

Once the sugar is dissolved, increase heat to high and bring to a boil, without stirring, until the caramel begins to brown. Lower the heat to medium-low and continue to cook, swirling pan occasionally, until the caramel turns a rich amber color.

Immediately stir in the pecans and pour onto the prepared baking sheet. Allow to cool. When completely cooled, chop into small pieces with a knife or pulse in a food processor. Store in an airtight container until ready to use. Yield: about 1½ cups.

For the Soufflé: Heat oven to 425 degrees. Butter 5 8-oz. ramekins.

In a large bowl, whisk together the egg yolks, banana, chocolate, and rum.

In the large bowl of an electric mixer using the whisk attachment, beat the egg whites and salt at medium speed until frothy. Increase speed to high and gradually beat in the sugar. Beat until stiff but not dry.

Stir into the yolk mixture ⅓ of the beaten egg whites and the praline. Gently fold in the remaining whites.

Divide batter among the prepared ramekins. Bake for 10 to 12 minutes, until puffed. Serve immediately with chocolate ice cream. Top with remaining praline, if you like. Yield: 5 servings.

Light Lemon-Raspberry Cake with White Chocolate Frosting

The bright flavors of fresh red raspberries and lemon zest shine in this cake.

CAKE

- 3½ cups cake flour, sifted
- ½ tsp. salt
- ½ tsp. baking powder
- ½ tsp. baking soda
- ¾ cup unsalted butter, room temperature, cut into pieces
- 2 cups granulated sugar
- ⅓ cup fresh lemon juice
- 1 generous tsp. fresh lemon zest
- 4 large eggs
- 1 cup plus 2 tbsp. buttermilk
- 2½ cups fresh red raspberries

FROSTING

- 11 oz. white chocolate, finely chopped
- 12 oz. cream cheese, room temperature, cut into pieces
- ¾ cup unsalted butter, room temperature, cut into pieces
- 2 tbsp. fresh lemon juice

Bev's Bites

This glorious cake can be made one day ahead. Cover with a cake dome and refrigerate; let stand at room temperature 1 hour before serving.

For the Cake: Heat oven to 350 degrees. Butter and flour 2 9"round cake pans with at least 2"-high sides. Line the bottom of the pans with rounds of parchment paper.

Sift together the cake flour, salt, baking powder, and baking soda into a medium bowl.

In the large bowl of an electric mixer, beat the butter until fluffy. Scrape down the sides of the bowl. Gradually add the sugar, beating until blended. Scrape down the sides of the bowl. Beat in the lemon juice and zest, then the eggs, one at a time, beating after each addition until well blended. Scrape down the sides of the bowl.

Alternate beating in dry ingredients with buttermilk in four batches. Gently fold in the berries. Divide batter evenly between cake pans.

Bake cakes until tester inserted into center comes out clean, 35 to 40 minutes. Cool cakes in pans on wire racks.

For the Frosting: Melt white chocolate; cool to lukewarm.

In the large bowl of an electric mixer, beat the cream cheese and butter until blended. Scrape down the sides of the bowl.

Beat in the lemon juice, then the cooled, melted white chocolate.

Turn cakes out onto a work surface and gently peel off parchment paper. Place one cake layer, flat side up, on serving platter. Spread with 1 cup of the frosting. Top with second cake layer, flat side down. Spread remaining frosting over top and sides of cake. Slice and serve. Yield: 10 to 12 servings.

A fork, a slice, and some additional fresh berries—nirvana!

All of these ingredients cost a few dollars at the grocery story. Digging in before these Peanut Butter Fudge Brownies are supposed to come out of the pan? Priceless.

Peanut Butter Fudge Brownies

A classic combo of flavors . . . it's lick-your-fingers good.

CHOCOLATE BATTER

2 cups granulated sugar
1 cup unsalted butter, room temperature, cut into pieces
4 large eggs
2 tsp. vanilla extract
1½ cups unbleached, all-purpose flour
¾ cup unsweetened cocoa powder, sifted
1 tsp. baking powder
½ tsp. salt
1 cup coarsely chopped semisweet chocolate

PEANUT BUTTER BATTER

¾ cup peanut butter
⅓ cup unsalted butter, room temperature, cut into pieces
⅓ cup granulated sugar
2 tbsp. unbleached, all-purpose flour
¾ tsp. vanilla extract
2 large eggs

FUDGE FROSTING

3 oz. unsweetened chocolate, coarsely chopped
3 tbsp. unsalted butter
2⅔ cups confectioners' sugar, sifted
¼ tsp. salt
¾ tsp. vanilla extract
4 to 5 tbsp. water

Heat oven to 350 degrees. Grease a 13" x 9" pan.

For the Chocolate Batter: In the large bowl of an electric mixer, beat the sugar and butter until light and fluffy. Add eggs, one at a time, beating well after each addition. Add vanilla and blend well. Scrape down the sides of the bowl.

In a small bowl, combine the flour, cocoa powder, baking powder, and salt. Gradually add the flour mixture to the sugar mixture; mix well. Stir in chocolate pieces. Set aside.

For the Peanut Butter Batter: Beat the peanut butter and butter in a small bowl with a handheld electric mixer until smooth. Add sugar and flour and mix well. Add vanilla and eggs; mix until well blended.

Spread half of the chocolate batter in prepared pan. Spread all of the peanut butter batter evenly over chocolate batter, then spread remaining chocolate batter evenly over peanut butter batter. To make a marbled effect, pull a knife through the layers in wide curves.

Bake for 35 to 45 minutes or until top springs back when touched lightly in center. Cool completely on wire rack.

For the Frosting: In a medium saucepan over low heat, melt chocolate with butter, stirring constantly until smooth. Remove saucepan from heat.

Whisk in confectioners' sugar, salt, and vanilla. Add enough water to make desired spreading consistency.

Frost cooled brownies. Yield: 36 brownies.

Chocolate Pairings

Chocolate-Orange Sorbet

Dairy free, this sorbet is a delightful alternative to chocolate ice cream.

4 cups water
⅔ cup granulated sugar
1½ tsp. instant coffee
½ cup fresh orange juice
1 tbsp. freshly grated orange zest
1 lb. bittersweet or semisweet chocolate, coarsely chopped

In a large saucepan over medium-high heat, bring the water, sugar, and instant coffee to a boil, stirring until sugar dissolves.

Mix in orange juice and zest. Reduce heat to low. Add the chocolate, whisking until smooth.

Transfer to a bowl and chill, uncovered, for 4 hours, stirring occasionally. Process sorbet mixture in an ice cream maker according to manufacturer's instructions, then transfer to a container, cover, and freeze for at least 6 hours and up to 3 days. Yield: 7 cups.

A chocolate fix, sorbet style.

Strawberry Sauté

This may be the quickest, easiest, and most delicious dessert you'll ever make!

3 tbsp. unsalted butter
¼ cup walnuts, coarsely chopped
3 tbsp. light brown sugar, firmly packed
2 cups fresh strawberries, halved or quartered
3 tbsp. grated semisweet or bittersweet chocolate
Vanilla frozen yogurt, for serving
¼ cup crumbled shortbread cookies, for serving

In a large nonstick skillet, melt butter just until bubbly. Add walnuts and cook, stirring briefly, until nuts begin to become fragrant and lightly browned.

Add brown sugar and stir until blended (less than 30 seconds).

Remove pan from heat. Add strawberries and chocolate. Quickly and gently stir to coat berries and melt chocolate.

Spoon over frozen yogurt and sprinkle with crumbled cookies. Yield: 4 servings.

Crazy Chocolate Cobbler with Seasonal Fresh Fruit

Cocoa powder added to the cobbler dough gives this dessert a rich flavor profile.

½ cup unsalted butter, melted
⅓ cup unsweetened cocoa powder, sifted
1 cup granulated sugar, divided
2 cups cake flour, sifted
2 tsp. baking powder
1 tsp. ground cinnamon
1 cup milk, whole or 2%
3 cups fresh seasonal fruit, such as sliced peaches, blackberries, nectarines, or plums
Freshly whipped cream, for serving

Heat oven to 350 degrees.

In a 3-quart baking dish, combine the butter, cocoa powder, and ¼ cup of the sugar.

In a medium bowl, combine the flour, baking powder, cinnamon, and remaining ¾ cup sugar. Add the milk and stir until the mixture is smooth. Spoon on top of the mixture already in the dish.

Sprinkle with the fresh fruit. Bake for 45 minutes or until a toothpick inserted in the center comes out clean. Let stand for 10 minutes, then top with freshly whipped cream and serve. Yield: 4 servings.

Chocolate Pairings

Layers of cheesecake goodness—and yes, it freezes beautifully as a make-ahead dessert for arriving company. (That is, if you can resist eating it!)

Favorite Flavors (Chocolate and Raspberry) Layered Cheesecake

When combining the cheesecake batter with the melted chocolate, make sure they're at the same temperature to result in a smooth batter. No one wants a lumpy cheesecake!

CRUST

1½ cups crushed graham cracker crumbs (about 11 full crackers)
¼ cup confectioners' sugar, sifted
⅓ cup plus 1 tbsp. unsalted butter, melted and cooled

FILLING

2 cups fresh raspberries, divided
½ tsp. granulated sugar
24 oz. cream cheese, room temperature, cut into pieces
14 oz. sweetened condensed milk
4 large eggs
1 tsp. vanilla extract
6 oz. semisweet chocolate, coarsely chopped, melted and cooled

Heat oven to 350 degrees.

For the Crust: Combine crumbs with confectioners' sugar, then stir in melted butter. Press onto the bottom and 1" to 2" up the sides of a 9" springform pan. Set aside.

For the Filling: In a small bowl, stir together 1 cup of the raspberries and sugar. Set aside.

In the large bowl of an electric mixer, beat the cream cheese and condensed milk until thoroughly combined. Scrape down the sides of the bowl.

Add eggs and vanilla and beat just until combined. Divide batter in half.

Stir melted chocolate into one portion of the batter. Pour chocolate batter into the crust-lined pan.

Stir raspberry mixture into the remaining portion of batter. Spoon raspberry batter over chocolate batter.

Place springform in a shallow baking pan to catch any drips. Pour ½" of water into the bottom of the baking pan so that springform pan rests in the water. Bake for 50 to 60 minutes or until center appears nearly set when shaken.

Remove springform pan from water bath and allow to cool on a wire rack for 15 minutes. Loosen crust from sides of the pan with a thin bladed knife and cool 30 additional minutes.

Remove sides of pan. Cool 1 hour, then cover and chill for at least 4 hours. Serve with remaining 1 cup raspberries. Yield: 12 to 16 servings.

Specks-of-Cranberry White Chocolate Yogurt Cheesecake

Yogurt cheese lightens up this bright, flavorful cheesecake.

YOGURT CHEESE

32 oz. container plain yogurt, nonfat, low-fat, or regular

CRUST

2 cups graham cracker crumbs
3 tbsp. unsalted butter, melted

CRANBERRY JAM

1¼ cup dried cranberries
½ cup granulated sugar
⅓ cup water
3 tbsp. fresh lemon juice

FILLING

4 oz. white chocolate, coarsely chopped
2 tbsp. milk, whole or 2%
1 tbsp. vanilla extract
1 cup granulated sugar
¼ cup cornstarch
¼ tsp. salt
8 oz. cream cheese, regular, or Neufchatel, room temperature, cut into pieces
8 oz. plain Greek yogurt
2 large eggs

For the Yogurt Cheese: Place a colander in a medium bowl and line colander with 2 layers of cheesecloth, allowing cheesecloth to extend over outside edge. Spoon yogurt into the colander. Cover loosely with plastic wrap and refrigerate for 12 hours.

Spoon the yogurt cheese from the colander into a bowl and discard liquid from the bowl underneath. Cover and refrigerate until ready to use.

For the Crust: Heat oven to 350 degrees.

Combine cracker crumbs and butter, tossing with a fork until moist. Press onto the bottom of a lightly greased 9" springform pan. Bake for 10 minutes, then cool on a wire rack.

Reduce oven to 300 degrees.

For the Cranberry Jam: In a medium saucepan, combine the cranberries, sugar, water, and lemon juice. Bring to a boil over medium-high heat.

Cover, reduce heat to medium-low, and simmer for 10 minutes or until cranberries are soft. Remove saucepan from heat and cool slightly.

Place cranberry mixture in a blender or food processor; pulse mixture until almost smooth. Set aside.

For the Filling: Place chocolate and milk in the top of a double boiler. Cook over simmering water until chocolate melts and mixture is smooth, stirring constantly. Remove from heat; stir in vanilla. Set aside.

In the large bowl of an electric mixer, combine the yogurt cheese, sugar, cornstarch, salt, cream cheese, and Greek yogurt and beat at low speed for 1 minute. Scrape down the sides of the bowl, then beat at medium speed until smooth, scraping bowl occasionally.

Beat in chocolate mixture. Add eggs one at a time, beating well after each addition. Scrape down the sides of the bowl. Beat an additional minute.

Fold in the cranberry jam and pour mixture over crust. Smooth top and loosely cover with foil.

Bake for 1 hour and 10 minutes. Turn oven off and remove foil from the top of the cheesecake. Let cheesecake rest in a closed oven for 1 hour and 15 minutes. Do not open the oven door or the heat will release.

Remove cheesecake from oven. Run a knife around the inside edge of the cheesecake in pan to loosen slightly. Cool to room temperature on a wire rack.

Cover and chill at least 8 hours before serving. Yield: 16 servings.

The perfect equilibrium—sweet white chocolate and tart cranberries.

Live and Let Chai Pots de Crème
Unique flavors and creamy texture are highlights of these pots.

⅔ cup heavy whipping cream
1 tsp. cardamom seeds, crushed or bruised (depending on how mean you're feeling!)
4 whole cloves
4 slices fresh ginger (about 2 tbsp. shredded), peeled
4½ oz. semisweet chocolate, finely chopped
1¼ cups milk, whole or 2%
3 tbsp. granulated sugar
1 large egg
3 large egg yolks
1 tsp. vanilla extract
Whipped cream, for garnish
Crystallized ginger, for garnish

Bev's Bites

Crushing or bruising the cardamom seeds is an important step to help release the essential oils and flavors. To do this, press the seeds with the flat plane of a chef's knife or the bottom of a heavy pan.

Position rack in lower part of oven and heat to 325 degrees. Lay a silicone liner or a double thickness of paper towels in a 13" x 9" baking pan. Set 6 6-8 oz. heatproof custard cups or ramekins in the pan.

In a medium saucepan, heat the cream, cardamom, cloves, and ginger over medium-high heat just until the mixture comes to a full boil. Remove from the heat and let stand for 30 minutes.

Place the chocolate in a heatproof bowl or large glass measuring cup. Reheat the cream mixture to a boil over medium heat. Immediately pour through a very fine sieve set over the chocolate, pressing down on the spices to extract as much flavor as possible. Let the chocolate stand, undisturbed, for 3 minutes, then gently stir until the chocolate melts completely and the mixture is well blended and smooth.

In a small saucepan, combine the milk and sugar and heat just until boiling, stirring until the sugar dissolves.

In a slow, thin stream, gradually stir about ⅔ of the boiling milk mixture into the chocolate mixture. If the chocolate begins to look oily and separated at any time, stop adding the milk and stir the chocolate until it is smooth again before continuing.

In a small bowl, whisk together the egg, egg yolks, and vanilla until well blended. Add the remaining ⅓ of the milk mixture to the eggs in a slow, thin stream, while constantly whisking.

Strain the egg-milk mixture through a fine sieve into the chocolate mixture; stir well to combine. Evenly divide among the custard cups, about ½ to ¾ cup each.

Place the pan on the oven rack and carefully add enough very hot water to come ¾" up the sides of the cups. Bake until the tops appear barely set when the cups are jiggled, about 18 to 20 minutes for smaller cups, 25 to 30 minutes for larger cups.

Transfer the cups to a wire rack and let cool thoroughly. Cover with plastic wrap and refrigerate until chilled, for at least 3 hours and up to 3 days.

Warm to room temperature for 30 minutes before serving. Garnish with a dollop of whipped cream and a piece of crystallized ginger. Yield: 6 servings.

Chocolate Pairings

A tropical twist to our chocolate island dream . . . catch any stowaways before this dessert disappears!

White Chocolate Mango Bread Pudding with Vanilla Ice Cream and Jane's Butterscotch Sauce

Layers upon layers of fabulous flavors make it difficult to decide what to taste first.

BREAD PUDDING

2 cups milk, whole or 2%
1¼ cups heavy whipping cream, divided
1 whole vanilla bean, slit down center
14 oz. sweetened condensed milk
12 oz. white chocolate, coarsely chopped
1 loaf of stale, artisan bread, cut into 1" cubes to equal 5 cups
4 large eggs
1 tbsp. ground cinnamon
1 cup granulated sugar, plus additional for sprinkling
2 ripe mangoes, plus additional for serving

JANE'S BUTTERSCOTCH SAUCE

6½ tbsp. unsalted butter, room temperature, cut into pieces
⅔ cup light corn syrup
1¼ cups light brown sugar, firmly packed
¾ cup evaporated milk

Vanilla ice cream, for serving

For the Bread Pudding: In a large saucepan, scald milk and 1 cup of the heavy cream with the vanilla bean. Add the sweetened condensed milk and white chocolate. Remove from heat and stir mixture until chocolate is melted and everything is combined.

In a large bowl, soak bread cubes in milk mixture for at least 1 hour at room temperature.

In a medium bowl, whisk together the eggs, cinnamon, and granulated sugar until all the sugar is dissolved. Add to soaking bread.

Cut mangoes into small cubes and stir into bread mixture.

Heat oven to 350 degrees.

Pour bread mixture into a well-buttered 4-quart baking dish. Pour the remaining ¼ cup heavy cream over the top and sprinkle with some additional granulated sugar.

Bake in the oven in a water bath for 1½ to 2 hours or until pudding rises and custard is set. Yield: 6 to 8 servings.

For Jane's Butterscotch Sauce: In a medium saucepan, cook the butter, corn syrup, and brown sugar over medium-high heat to the soft ball stage (238 degrees on a candy thermometer). Remove from heat and cool slightly. Whisk in evaporated milk until smooth. Yield: about 1½ cups.

To serve, top warm bread pudding with vanilla ice cream and Jane's Butterscotch Sauce.

Jane's Butterscotch Sauce, from Bev Shaffer, *Cakes to Die For!* (Gretna, LA: Pelican, 2010). Reprinted by permission of the publisher.

Warm Chocolate Raspberry Pudding Cake

One of the few things better than eating a chocolate cake is having a chocolate cake filled with raspberry flavor and eating it warm.

FROSTING

½ cup seedless raspberry jam
½ cup heavy whipping cream
3 oz. bittersweet chocolate, coarsely chopped

CAKE

½ cup boiling water
⅓ cup plus 2 tsp. unsweetened cocoa powder, not Dutch process, sifted
¼ cup whole milk
½ tsp. vanilla extract
⅓ cup seedless raspberry jam
½ cup unsalted butter, room temperature, cut into pieces
⅓ cup light brown sugar, firmly packed
⅓ cup granulated sugar
2 large eggs
1 cup unbleached, all-purpose flour
¾ tsp. baking soda
¼ tsp. salt
Red raspberries, for garnish

Bev's Bites

Cake may be made 1 day ahead, cooled completely, and left in the pan. Cover and store at room temperature. When ready to serve, reheat cake, uncovered, at 350 degrees for 10 to 15 minutes.

Heat oven to 350 degrees. Generously butter a 9" x 2" round cake pan.

For the Frosting: In a small saucepan, bring the jam, cream, and chocolate to a simmer, stirring occasionally, until smooth.

Pour into buttered cake pan. Set aside.

For the Cake: In a medium bowl, whisk together the boiling water and cocoa powder until smooth. Whisk in milk, vanilla, and jam.

In the large bowl of an electric mixer, beat together the butter, brown sugar, and granulated sugar until light and fluffy. Scrape down the sides of the bowl. Add eggs, one at a time, beating well after each addition.

In a medium bowl, sift together the flour, baking soda, and salt. Alternate adding the flour mixture to the egg mixture with the cocoa mixture, beginning and ending with the flour mixture. Beat well after each addition. Scrape down the sides of the bowl.

Pour batter evenly over frosting mixture in the cake pan and bake 30 to 35 minutes or until a tester inserted into cake comes out clean (remember that frosting on the bottom will still be liquid).

Cool cake slightly in pan on a rack, 10 to 20 minutes.

Run a thin knife around the edge of the pan to loosen cake. Invert a cake plate with a slight lip over cake pan and, holding pan and plate together with both hands, invert cake onto plate.

Frosting will spill over the sides of the cake and run onto the plate. Serve cake garnished with raspberries. Yield: 6 to 8 servings.

Unfortunately, this paper does not taste as good as the cake itself—please remove your fork from this page! Looks like you'll have to get baking . . .

Espresso your love for these biscotti by sharing them with your friends.

White Chocolate Chocolate Biscotti

Serve these with sparkling wine or a sweet dessert wine for something special.

3 cups unbleached, all-purpose flour
¾ cup granulated sugar
⅓ cup light brown sugar, firmly packed
1 tbsp. baking powder
¾ tsp. salt
3 oz. unsweetened chocolate, melted and cooled
3 large eggs
⅓ cup light olive oil
2 tbsp. fresh orange juice
1 tbsp. freshly grated orange zest
2 tbsp. Grand Marnier
1 tsp. vanilla extract
1 cup semisweet chocolate chips
1 cup walnut pieces, lightly toasted
12 oz. white chocolate, coarsely chopped
1 tbsp. vegetable shortening

Heat oven to 350 degrees. Line two baking sheets with parchment paper or silicone liners.

In a large bowl, combine the flour, granulated sugar, brown sugar, baking powder, and salt.

Add the melted, unsweetened chocolate, eggs, oil, orange juice and zest, Grand Marnier, and vanilla and stir well to combine.

Add chocolate chips and nuts; mix until dough is well blended.

Quarter the dough. Shape into 4 logs, each about 2½" wide and 8" long. (The logs should be flat on the bottom and rounded on the top.) Place two logs on each of the two prepared baking sheets.

Bake until just firm to the touch, about 20 minutes. Cool logs for 10 minutes on the baking sheets. Using a serrated knife, cut diagonally into ½"-wide slices. Place slices, cut side down, on the pans and bake until crisp, about 15 additional minutes. Cool cookies on a wire rack.

In a double boiler, melt white chocolate and shortening over barely simmering water, stirring until smooth.

Dip one end of each cookie about 1" into white chocolate to coat. Lay cookies on waxed paper-lined cookie sheets and allow to set until white chocolate is firm (you may chill to speed process).

Serve immediately or wrap airtight and store for up to 2 days, freezing for longer storage. Yield: 3 dozen biscotti.

Chocolate Pairings

Chocolate Pepita Shortbread Stars

Are the same old cookies driving you nuts? These shortbread stars with pumpkin seeds will satisfy, and the cookie dough is extremely easy to work with. What a fiesta!

¾ cup unsalted, shelled pepitas (pumpkin seeds), toasted
4 oz. semisweet chocolate, coarsely chopped
1 cup unsalted butter, room temperature, cut into pieces
½ cup plus 2 tbsp. granulated sugar, divided
¾ tsp. ground cinnamon
¼ tsp. salt
2¼ cups unbleached, all-purpose flour
1 large egg white, lightly whisked

Heat oven to 325 degrees.

Grind pepitas in a coffee grinder, blender, or food processor until coarsely ground; set aside.

Melt chocolate, then transfer to a large bowl and allow to cool slightly.

In the large bowl of an electric mixer, combine the butter, ½ cup of the sugar, ground cinnamon, salt, and melted chocolate. Beat until well blended.

Add flour and ground pepitas, stirring just until blended.

Roll out dough on a floured surface to ½" thickness. Using a 3" star cookie cutter lightly dipped in flour, cut out cookies. Transfer to ungreased baking sheets, spacing 1" apart. Reroll dough scraps and use to cut out additional cookies. Try not to reroll dough more than once.

Brush cookies with egg white and sprinkle with remaining 2 tbsp. sugar.

Bake cookies until just firm to the touch, about 15 to 18 minutes. Cool 5 minutes on baking sheets, then transfer to a wire rack to cool completely. Yield: 1½ dozen cookies.

Pepitas and chocolate star in these thick, shortbread cookies—olé!

Fudgy Goes Latin Bars

Dulce de Leche and chocolate combine for a sweet something of a bar.

SHORTBREAD

½ cup unsalted butter, room temperature, cut into pieces
⅓ cup light brown sugar, firmly packed
½ tsp. vanilla extract
½ tsp. salt
1 cup unbleached, all-purpose flour

DULCE DE LECHE

1 cup heavy whipping cream
1 cup dark brown sugar, firmly packed
½ cup sweetened condensed milk

CHOCOLATE DULCE DE LECHE

1 cup heavy whipping cream
1 cup Dulce de Leche
4 large egg yolks
5 oz. bittersweet chocolate, finely chopped

Bev's Bites

The regular Dulce de Leche may be made 1 day ahead. Cover and chill; rewarm over medium low heat just until warm and pourable when ready to use.

For the Shortbread: Heat oven to 375 degrees. Butter a 9" square cake pan, then line the bottom and two sides with foil, leaving an overhang. Gently butter foil.

In a medium bowl, blend together the butter, brown sugar, vanilla, and salt. Sift in the flour, and blend with a fork until a soft dough forms.

Pat and spread dough evenly in prepared pan using an offset spatula, clean fingertips, or the back of a spoon, then prick all over with a fork.

Bake until golden, 15 to 20 minutes, then allow to cool completely in the pan on a wire rack.

For the Dulce de Leche: In a medium saucepan, combine the cream and brown sugar. Stir over medium heat until sugar dissolves. Boil until mixture is reduced to 1 cup, stirring occasionally, about 10 to 20 minutes. Stir in sweetened condensed milk. Set aside. Yield: 1⅓ cups.

For the Chocolate Dulce de Leche: In a medium saucepan, bring the cream and Dulce de Leche to a simmer, stirring until well blended.

In a medium bowl, whisk together the egg yolks, then slowly whisk in 1 cup of the hot cream mixture.

Return to pan and cook over medium heat, stirring constantly, until pan is visible in the tracks of the spoon and mixture registers 170 degrees on an instant-read thermometer. Remove saucepan from heat and whisk in chocolate until melted.

Pour chocolate mixture over cooled shortbread and chill, uncovered, until cold and set, about 2½ hours.

Run a small knife around edges to loosen, then transfer to a cutting board using foil to help lift and carry the bars. With a hot, clean knife, cut into 24 bars. Chill until ready to serve. Yield: 24 bars.

Chocolate-Caramel Drizzled Oranges

Simple and sublime . . . fresh oranges pair well with the sweet drizzle of caramel and chocolate caramel. How easy!

4 medium seedless oranges
¼ cup unsalted butter, room temperature
¾ cup light brown sugar, firmly packed
1 tbsp. light corn syrup
¼ cup milk, whole or 2%
¼ cup semisweet chocolate, finely chopped
¼ cup finely chopped walnuts, toasted, optional

Peel oranges and remove white membranes.

Slice each orange into 4 or 5 round slices; set aside.

Melt butter in a small saucepan. Add brown sugar and corn syrup and bring mixture to a boil, stirring constantly, until sugar is dissolved.

Gradually add milk to boiling caramel mixture, stirring constantly. Remove from heat.

Pour a ½ cup of the caramel mixture into a glass measuring cup. Chill for 30 minutes.

To the remaining caramel mixture, add chopped chocolate, stirring until melted. Chill for 20 minutes.

Arrange orange slices on 4 serving plates. Drizzle each serving with some of the caramel mixture and top with some of the chocolate caramel mixture.

Sprinkle each plate with walnuts, if using. Serve immediately. Yield: 4 servings.

Chocolate Chip Biscuits with Mangoes and Pineapple

There's nothing ordinary about these chocolate chip biscuits.

BISCUITS

2 cups unbleached, all-purpose flour
½ cup granulated sugar
1 tbsp. baking powder
½ tsp. salt
½ cup unsalted butter, room temperature, cut into pieces
¼ cup shortening
⅔ cup heavy whipping cream
½ cup semisweet chocolate, coarsely chopped

FILLING

1⅓ cups heavy whipping cream, chilled
3 tbsp. confectioners' sugar
1 tsp. vanilla extract

TOPPING

2 mangoes, pitted, peeled, largely diced
1½ cups fresh pineapple chunks

For the Biscuits: Heat oven to 400 degrees.

In a large bowl, combine the flour, sugar, baking powder, and salt. Cut in butter and shortening until crumbly.

With a fork, stir in heavy cream just until moistened. Stir in the chocolate.

Turn dough out onto lightly floured surface and knead lightly just until smooth. Roll dough to ¾" thickness. Using a 2½" scalloped round cutter, cut out 8 biscuits.

Place 1" apart on a cookie sheet and bake for 10 to 14 minutes or until lightly browned.

For the Filling: In the large bowl of an electric mixer, beat the chilled cream at high speed with the whisk attachment, scraping bowl often, until soft peaks form. Continue beating, gradually adding confectioners' sugar and vanilla, until stiff peaks form.

To serve, split biscuits and place on individual dessert plates. Spoon filling on bottom half of biscuits, then place mango pieces on whipped cream. Top with remaining half of biscuits and spoon pineapple over biscuits. Yield: 8 servings.

Chocolate Chip Pumpkin Cheesecake with Chocolate-Cookie Crust

Allow the flavors to meld by making this rich pumpkin dessert a day ahead of serving.

CRUST

1½ cups crème-filled chocolate sandwich cookies (about 19 cookies), crushed
2 tbsp. unsalted butter, softened

FILLING

24 oz. cream cheese, room temperature, cut into pieces
1 cup granulated sugar
3 tbsp. unbleached, all-purpose flour
2 tsp. ground cinnamon
1 tbsp. ginger, freshly grated
½ tsp. ground cloves
1 cup pumpkin purée
4 large eggs
1½ cups mini semisweet chocolate chips

Heat oven to 325 degrees.

For the Crust: In a medium bowl, combine the cookie crumbs and butter; mix well. Press in bottom and up sides of an ungreased 9" springform pan. Refrigerate.

For the Filling: In the large bowl of an electric mixer, beat cream cheese, sugar, flour, cinnamon, ginger, and cloves until smooth. Scrape down the sides of the bowl. Add the pumpkin and eggs, beating just until combined. Stir in chocolate chips and pour batter into crust-lined pan.

Bake for 60 minutes or until edges are set (center of cheesecake will still be soft). Turn oven off and let cheesecake stand in oven for 30 minutes or until center is set.

Remove from oven, place on a wire rack, and cool to room temperature. Run a knife around the inside edge of springform pan to loosen cheesecake. Refrigerate overnight. Yield: 12 servings.

White Chocolate Mousse Tart with Fresh Blueberry Topping

Easily made ahead, this mousse tart can be quickly garnished with white chocolate confetti or shavings just before serving.

TART CRUST

1¼ cups unbleached, all-purpose flour
⅓ cup confectioners' sugar, sifted
½ tsp. salt
½ cup plus 2 tbsp. unsalted butter, chilled, cut into pieces
2 large egg yolks
1 tbsp. water, cold

FILLING

1 tbsp. water
3 tbsp. fresh lemon juice
1 tsp. unflavored gelatin
1 cup heavy whipping cream, chilled, divided
4 oz. white chocolate, finely chopped

FRESH BLUEBERRY TOPPING

3 cups fresh blueberries, divided
3 tbsp. fresh lemon juice
3 tbsp. granulated sugar

White chocolate confetti or shavings, for garnish

Bev's Bites

May be made 1 day ahead, if refrigerated.

For the Crust: In a food processor, mix together the flour, sugar, and salt. Add butter and pulse until mixture resembles coarse meal.

In a small bowl, mix together the egg yolks and water. Add to the flour mixture and process just until moist clumps form. Gather dough into a ball, flatten into a disk, and refrigerate for 1 hour.

Heat oven to 350 degrees.

Roll out tart crust on floured work surface to a 13" round. Transfer to a 9"-diameter tart pan with removable bottom, pressing gently in place. Trim dough overhang to ½". Lift overhang over itself and press firmly into the tart, forming double thick sides. Freeze for 15 minutes.

Line crust with foil and fill with dried beans. Bake until sides are set, about 15 minutes. Gently remove foil and beans and prick crust all over with a fork. Bake until crust is golden brown and baked through, about 15 to 18 minutes. Transfer to wire rack and cool crust completely.

For the Filling: In a small saucepan, combine the water and lemon juice. Do not heat. Sprinkle gelatin over liquid. Let stand 10 minutes to allow gelatin to soften, then stir over low heat until gelatin dissolves. Set aside.

In a medium saucepan, bring ¼ cup of cream to a simmer. Remove saucepan from heat and add white chocolate, stirring until smooth. Whisk in gelatin mixture, then refrigerate just until cool and beginning to thicken slightly, about 10 minutes, stirring often.

In the large bowl of an electric mixer, beat the remaining ¾ cup cream until stiff peaks form. Gently fold in white chocolate mixture. Spoon mousse into crust, smooth top, and refrigerate until set, about 2 hours.

For the Topping: Finely chop ½ cup of the blueberries in a food processor, then transfer to a medium saucepan. Add lemon juice and sugar and stir over medium heat until mixture boils and thickens slightly. Remove saucepan from heat. Stir in remaining blueberries and allow to cool.

Spoon blueberry topping over mousse, covering completely. Refrigerate until cold, about 1 hour.

When ready to serve, remove tart from pan and transfer to a serving platter. Sprinkle with white chocolate confetti or shavings and cut into wedges. Yield: 8 servings.

Chocolate-with-a-Hint-of-Orange Bread Pudding

It is amazing how simple bread pudding is yet how good it tastes. This version packs a full chocolate flavor with a hint of orange.

4 cups artisan white bread cubes, fresh or stale
2 cups milk, whole or 2%
½ cup granulated sugar
3 oz. bittersweet chocolate, coarsely chopped
4 large eggs, lightly beaten
1 tbsp. fresh orange zest, finely shredded
1 tsp. vanilla extract
⅛ tsp. salt

Heat oven to 325 degrees.

Place the bread cubes in a buttered 2-quart square baking dish. Set aside.

In a medium saucepan, combine the milk, sugar, and chocolate. Cook over medium heat until chocolate melts, whisking frequently. Remove saucepan from heat.

In a medium bowl, combine the eggs, orange zest, vanilla, and salt. Gradually whisk in the chocolate mixture, then pour mixture over bread in the baking dish. Press lightly with the back of a spoon to moisten all bread cubes.

Bake, uncovered, for 35 to 40 minutes or until evenly puffed and set. Cool about 30 minutes; serve warm. Yield: 6 to 8 servings.

Fudgy Brownies with Chocolate-Cinnamon Mousse

I'd say don't gild the lily, but with a combination like this one, how can I resist?

CHOCOLATE CINNAMON MOUSSE

1 cup heavy whipping cream
4 cinnamon sticks, broken in half
¼ cup hot cocoa mix

BROWNIES

6 oz. unsweetened chocolate, coarsely chopped
2 oz. bittersweet chocolate, coarsely chopped
1 cup unsalted butter, room temperature, cut into pieces
3 cups granulated sugar
6 large eggs, lightly beaten
1½ tsp. vanilla extract
1¾ cups unbleached, all-purpose flour
½ tsp. salt
2 cups large pecan pieces, lightly toasted, then coarsely chopped

For the Chocolate-Cinnamon Mousse: In a medium saucepan, bring the cream and cinnamon sticks to a simmer. Be sure not to boil the liquid. Remove saucepan from heat and allow mixture to steep for 1 hour at room temperature.

Cover and refrigerate cinnamon cream overnight. Strain mixture into the large bowl of an electric mixer. Whisk in hot cocoa mix. Beat mixture until soft peaks form. Yield: 2¼ cups.

For the Brownies: Heat oven to 350 degrees. Lightly grease a 15" x 10" jellyroll pan.

In a large saucepan, combine both chocolates and butter. Set over low heat, stirring often to prevent scorching, until chocolates and butter are melted and smooth.

Remove saucepan from heat and stir in sugar until well blended.

When mixture is cool enough to touch, stir in eggs and vanilla. Blend in flour and salt. Gently stir in pecans.

Spread mixture into prepared pan and bake for 18 to 22 minutes or until a toothpick inserted in the center comes out with a few moist crumbs attached. Cool completely in the pan on a wire rack.

Cut brownies into portions and dollop a portion of the mousse on top or beside the brownies before serving. Yield: 24 brownies.

Chocolate Pairings

Fudge Cake with Warm Ganache and Raspberry Jam Topping

Simply decadent, easy-to-make 1-layer cake.

CAKE

1 cup unbleached, all-purpose flour
¼ cup plus 2 tbsp. unsweetened cocoa powder, not Dutch process, sifted
½ tsp. baking soda
¼ tsp. salt
½ cup unsalted butter, melted and warm
1¼ cups light brown sugar, firmly packed
2 large eggs
1 tsp. vanilla extract
½ cup hot water
1 cup seedless red raspberry jam

WARM GANACHE

8 oz. bittersweet chocolate, finely chopped
1 cup heavy whipping cream
1 tbsp. granulated sugar

For the Cake: Heat oven to 350 degrees and position rack in lower third of oven. Grease the bottom only of an 8" round cake pan or line with a circle of parchment paper.

In a small bowl, whisk the flour, cocoa powder, baking soda, and salt.

In a large bowl, combine the butter and brown sugar. Add the eggs and vanilla, stirring until well blended.

Add the flour mixture all at once and stir just until all the flour is moistened. Pour the hot water over the batter; stir only until it is incorporated and smooth. Scrape the batter into the prepared pan.

Bake for 25 to 30 minutes or until a toothpick inserted in the center comes out clean. Let cool in pan on a wire rack for 20 minutes, then run a thin knife around the inside edge of pan and invert the cake onto the rack. Gently peel off the parchment paper. Invert it again onto the rack (it should be right-side up) and let cool completely.

Once cake is cool, set the rack over a baking sheet lined with waxed paper.

In a small saucepan, warm the raspberry jam, beating well to create a smooth, spreadable mixture. Gently spread jam on top of cooled cake. Allow to rest for 30 minutes.

For the Ganache: Put the chocolate in a medium-size, heat-proof bowl.

In a small saucepan, bring the cream and sugar to a boil and immediately pour hot cream over the chocolate. Whisk gently until the chocolate is completely melted and smooth. Allow to cool slightly, about 30 minutes, before using.

Pour the warm ganache over the cake and use an angled icing spatula to gently spread it over the top of the cake and down the sides. Let set before serving, about 1 hour. Yield: 8 to 10 servings.

Chocolate-Caramel Tart with Drunken Raspberries and Whipped Cream

Sophisticated enough for a special occasion or an everyday feast.

CRUST

1 cup unbleached, all-purpose flour
3 tbsp. granulated sugar
½ tsp. salt
½ cup unsalted butter, chilled, cut into pieces
2 large egg yolks
3 tbsp. cocoa nibs

CARAMEL FILLING

1 cup granulated sugar
¼ cup water
¼ cup heavy whipping cream
4 tbsp. unsalted butter, cut into 4 pieces
½ vanilla bean, split lengthwise
¼ tsp. fleur de sel, finely ground

GANACHE

1 cup heavy whipping cream
5 oz. bittersweet chocolate, chopped

DRUNKEN RASPBERRIES

1 pint fresh red raspberries
¾ cup raspberry liqueur

Freshly whipped cream, for serving

Bev's Bites

Can be made 2 days ahead through the ganache. Refrigerate, covered, once chocolate is firm.

For the Crust: Heat oven to 375 degrees and place rack in center of oven. Lightly grease a 9" tart pan with removable bottom.

In a food processor, blend the flour, sugar, and salt. Add butter and pulse until mixture resembles coarse meal. Add egg yolks and pulse until moist crumbs form. Add cocoa nibs and pulse until incorporated.

Press dough onto bottom and sides of prepared pan. Line with foil and weigh with dried beans. Bake for 10 minutes, then carefully remove beans and foil. Continue to bake for about 10 additional minutes or until crust is golden brown. Cool in pan on wire rack while preparing filling.

For the Caramel Filling: In a medium saucepan, combine sugar and water. Stir over medium-low heat until sugar dissolves. Increase heat to high and boil without stirring until mixture is deep amber, occasionally brushing down sides of pan with a wet pastry brush to incorporate sugar crystals and swirling pan, about 10 minutes. Remove from heat; add cream (be careful—mixture will bubble vigorously).

Add butter and stir over low heat until caramel is completely smooth. Scrape in seeds from vanilla bean; stir in fleur de sel. Cool 10 minutes. Pour warm caramel into crust. Let stand at room temperature until completely cool, about 1 hour.

For the Ganache: In a small saucepan, bring cream to a simmer. Remove saucepan from heat; add chocolate. Whisk until smooth. Let stand until slightly cooled but still pourable, about 10 minutes. Pour evenly over filling. Refrigerate tart, uncovered, until chocolate is firm, about 2 hours.

For the Drunken Raspberries: Combine raspberries and liqueur in a small bowl. Let macerate at room temperature for at least 1 and up to 3 hours.

When ready to serve, cut tart into thin slices. Arrange slices on serving plate and spoon some berries and whipped cream on top. Yield: 10 to 12 servings.

White Chocolate and Raspberry Bread Pudding with White Chocolate Sauce and a Raspberry Sauce

A rich and decadent rendition of a classic.

BREAD PUDDING

- 2 cups heavy whipping cream
- ½ cup plus 3 tbsp. granulated sugar, divided
- ½ vanilla bean, split lengthwise
- 3 large eggs, lightly beaten
- 8 oz. fresh French baguette, cut into ½" squares
- 1 pint fresh raspberries, divided, plus additional for serving
- 4 oz. white chocolate, coarsely chopped
- 1 tbsp. unsalted butter, room temperature

WHITE CHOCOLATE SAUCE

- 2 cups white chocolate, coarsely chopped
- ¾ cup heavy whipping cream
- 1 tbsp. plus 1 tsp. light corn syrup

RASPBERRY SAUCE

- 8 cups fresh raspberries
- 1¼ cups granulated sugar
- 1 tbsp. fresh lemon juice

Bev's Bites

Remember, when it comes to white chocolate, I only have two words to say: *cocoa* and *butter*. Cocoa butter *must* be in the ingredients, otherwise you've bought yourself a sickeningly sweet vanilla confectioners' coating. Again, as with all chocolates, only the best will do!

For the Bread Pudding: In a medium saucepan, combine the cream and ½ cup of the sugar over medium heat. Scrape the vanilla bean seeds into the cream mixture and add the whole vanilla bean. Bring the mixture to a simmer, then immediately remove the saucepan from heat. Set aside until the mixture is cool enough to touch.

Whisk the eggs into the cooled cream mixture and set aside to cool completely.

In a large bowl, combine bread cubes, ¾ of the berries, and the chopped white chocolate. Stir in the cooled cream mixture. Allow the mixture to stand at room temperature for 1 hour.

Heat oven to 350 degrees. Lightly grease an 8" x 8" baking dish with butter. Sprinkle the remaining 3 tbsp. of the sugar into the dish and tap lightly until the bottom and sides of the baking dish are evenly coated.

Spoon the bread pudding mixture into the prepared dish, pouring any remaining custard over the top of the pudding. (The mixture will be very loose at this point.)

Place the remaining raspberries on top of the pudding. Cover the pan with foil and set inside a larger baking dish. Fill the larger pan with enough water to come halfway up the sides of the pudding. Bake for 30 minutes.

Increase oven to 375 degrees and remove the foil from the top of the pudding. Bake 35 to 40 minutes or until the top is golden brown. Remove the pudding from the water bath and set aside to cool slightly.

For the White Chocolate Sauce: Combine the chocolate and cream in the top of a double boiler and set over barely simmering water. Whisk the chocolate cream mixture until the chocolate is melted and mixture is smooth.

Remove the sauce from the heat and stir in the corn syrup. Set aside to cool to room temperature. Yield: 3 cups.

For the Raspberry Sauce: In a medium saucepan, combine the raspberries, sugar, and lemon juice and cook over medium heat. Bring mixture to a boil, stirring occasionally, until sugar is dissolved. Reduce heat to medium-low and cook,stirring occasionally, for 5 minutes. Remove from heat and cool slightly.

Place mixture into the container of a Vitamix blender and secure the lid. Select Variable 1. Slowly increase speed to Variable 10, then to High. Use the tamper as needed to keep mixture flowing. Blend for 1 minute or until desired consistency is reached. Yield: 1½ cups.

When ready to serve, cut the cooled bread pudding into nine equal squares. Serve each portion lightly drizzled with white chocolate sauce, raspberry sauce, and a few additional berries. Yield: 9 servings.

Red, White, and Chocolate Holiday Tart

This is my favorite go-to holiday dessert, with outstanding colors and equally outstanding flavors.

RED TOPPING

½ cup 100% cranberry juice, divided
1 tsp. unflavored gelatin
12 oz. fresh cranberries
¾ cup granulated sugar
2 tsp. fresh lemon juice
1 tsp. lemon zest, freshly grated
1 tsp. ginger, freshly grated
1 tsp. crystallized ginger, finely chopped
Pinch of salt

CHOCOLATE CRUST

1¼ cups chocolate cookie crumbs (made from about 6½ oz. cookies)
¼ cup granulated sugar
⅛ tsp. salt
6 tbsp. unsalted butter, melted, divided

WHITE FILLING

8 oz. mascarpone cheese
½ cup confectioners' sugar, sifted
½ cup heavy whipping cream, cold
1 tsp. vanilla extract

JEWEL-LIKE SUGARED CRANBERRIES

¼ cup water
¾ cup granulated sugar, divided
½ cup fresh cranberries

Bev's Bites

The red topping may be made up to two days ahead if covered and kept in the refrigerator.

The sugared cranberries work best if someone else makes them for you and you sit and watch! It's important to test one or two just to be sure that they are delicious (but save some for the finished tart, please).

For the Red Topping: Pour ¼ cup of the cranberry juice into a small bowl and sprinkle gelatin over the top. Let stand until the gelatin softens, about 15 minutes.

In a medium saucepan over medium-high heat, combine remaining ¼ cup cranberry juice, fresh cranberries, sugar, lemon juice and zest, grated and crystallized ginger, and salt. Bring to a boil, stirring until sugar dissolves. Reduce heat to medium; simmer until cranberries are tender but still plump, about 5 minutes. Strain into medium bowl. Set cranberries aside.

Add gelatin mixture to hot juice in bowl; stir until gelatin dissolves. Stir cranberries back into juice. Chill until cranberry mixture is cold and slightly thickened, at least 8 hours or overnight.

For the Chocolate Crust: Heat oven to 350 degrees.

In a medium bowl, combine the cookie crumbs, sugar, and salt. Add 5 tbsp. of the melted butter and stir until crumbs feel moist when pressed together with fingertips. Add the remaining 1 tbsp. melted butter. Press crumb mixture firmly onto bottom and up sides of a 9" tart pan with removable bottom.

Bake until crust begins to set and is slightly crisp, about 14 minutes. If the crust puffs while baking, press down with a spoon and continue baking. Transfer tart pan to a wire rack and cool crust completely before filling.

For the White Filling: In a medium bowl, whisk together the mascarpone, confectioners' sugar, cream, and vanilla until just thick enough to spread. Be careful not to overbeat as the mixture may curdle.

Spread filling in cooled crust.

Spoon red topping (cranberry mixture) evenly over white (mascarpone) filling. Chill for at least 2 hours and up to 6 hours.

For the Jewel-Like Sugared Cranberries: In a small saucepan, bring the water and ½ cup of the sugar to a boil, stirring until sugar has dissolved. Simmer uncovered for 2 minutes. Remove saucepan from heat.

Put the remaining ¼ cup sugar in a small bowl. Lightly brush cranberries with sugar syrup, then immediately roll in sugar. Transfer to a wax paper-lined baking sheet. Allow to dry at room temperature for 2 to 3 hours. (Try not to eat too many "testers.") They'll keep, chilled in one layer on a baking pan, uncovered, for 3 days.

When ready to serve, garnish the tart with sugared cranberries and slice into segments. Yield: 8 to 10 servings.

IT'S A PARTY!

Can't decide which Devil's Food Cupcake to grab? Have one of each and tell everyone, "The devil made me do it!"

When it comes to chocolate, there is never a bad reason to throw a party. So, think of a reason (any one at all—no need to be serious), pick your recipes, invite your guests, and have a chocolate party!

Brownie Chunk Cookies

Baking bonus: you will need only half of this batch of brownies to make the cookies! Leftovers never tasted so sweet . . .

BROWNIES

5 oz. unsweetened chocolate, coarsely chopped
½ cup unsalted butter, cut into pieces
2 cups granulated sugar
2 tsp. vanilla extract
4 large eggs
¼ tsp. salt
1 cup unbleached, all purpose-flour

COOKIES

2½ cups unbleached, all-purpose flour
1 tsp. baking soda
¼ tsp. salt
1 cup unsalted butter, room temperature, cut into pieces
1 cup light brown sugar, firmly packed
½ cup granulated sugar
2 large eggs
1 tsp. vanilla extract
1 cup walnut pieces, lightly toasted

For the Brownies: Heat oven to 350 degrees. Line a 13" x 9" baking pan with foil, leaving an overhang. Lightly grease the foil.

In a large saucepan, stir together the chocolate and butter over low heat until melted and smooth. Cool 15 minutes.

Whisk sugar and vanilla into chocolate mixture, then whisk in the eggs and salt until blended. Stir in the flour. Spread batter into prepared pan.

Bake brownies until a tester inserted in the center comes out with moist crumbs attached, about 15 to 20 minutes. Cool in pan on wire rack. Cover and chill overnight.

Using foil as an aid, lift brownie sheet from pan and cut in half. Set half the brownies aside (or eat—who are we kidding). Slice half the brownies into ½" cubes.

For the Cookies: Heat oven to 350 degrees. Line two rimmed baking sheets with parchment paper or silicone liners.

In a medium bowl, whisk together the flour, baking soda, and salt.

In the large bowl of an electric mixer, beat the butter, brown sugar, and granulated sugar until smooth. Beat in eggs and vanilla. Stir in flour mixture. Scrape down the sides of the bowl. Mix until well blended.

Gently stir in walnuts. Fold in brownie cubes (don't panic if some of the brownies crumble . . . just be gentle!).

Lightly spray a ¼- to ⅓-cup ice cream scoop with nonstick cooking spray. Scoop batter and drop onto prepared baking sheets, spacing about 2" apart and spraying scoop as needed.

Using moist fingertips, gently flatten mounds to 1" thickness. Bake cookies, one sheet at a time, until golden, about 15 to 18 minutes. Cool cookies on wire racks. Yield: 18 cookies.

It's a Party!

Chocolate and More Chocolate Mini Cupcakes

These bite-size treats are ready for you to pop in your mouth at party time!

CUPCAKES

½ cup granulated sugar
¼ cup unsalted butter, room temperature, cut into pieces
½ tsp. ground cinnamon
¼ cup buttermilk
1 oz. unsweetened chocolate, melted
1 large egg
1 tsp. vanilla extract
1 cup unbleached, all-purpose flour
1 tsp. baking soda
¼ tsp. salt
¼ cup boiling water

FROSTING

⅓ cup unsalted butter, room temperature
¼ tsp. ground cinnamon
1 oz. unsweetened chocolate, melted
2 cups confectioners' sugar, sifted
⅓ cup heavy whipping cream

For the Cupcakes: Heat oven to 350 degrees. Place 30 foil or paper baking cups into mini muffin tins. Set aside.

In the large bowl of an electric mixer, beat the sugar and butter until light and fluffy. Scrape down the sides of the bowl. Add cinnamon, buttermilk, chocolate, egg, and vanilla; continue beating until well mixed.

Reduce speed to low and add the flour, baking soda, and salt. Beat until well blended. Add the boiling water and continue beating until smooth.

Spoon about 1 tbsp. of batter into each prepared muffin pan cup. Bake for 10 to 12 minutes or until a toothpick inserted in the center comes out clean. Cool completely. Yield: 30 mini cupcakes.

For the Frosting: In the large bowl of an electric mixer, beat the butter, cinnamon, and chocolate on medium speed until creamy. Scrape down the sides of the bowl. Alternate gradually adding confectioners' sugar with heavy cream and beating well after each addition until creamy.

Pipe or frost each cupcake with about 1 tbsp. of frosting. Yield: enough for one batch of mini cupcakes.

Batter . . .

Bake
Test
Cool
Frost
Yum!

Chocolate Sushi = Chocolate Party!

Chocolate Sushi

Party participation is a must for this chocolate sushi. What fun!

MODELING CHOCOLATE

12 oz. semisweet chocolate, coarsely chopped
2 oz. light corn syrup

STICKY RICE

1 cup sushi rice, rinsed
2 cups apple juice

Fresh baby spinach or basil leaves
Seasonal fruits, julienned

For the Modeling Chocolate: Melt the chocolate, then add the corn syrup and mix thoroughly. Wrap mixture in plastic wrap and refrigerate for 2 hours.

For the Sticky Rice: In a medium saucepan, combine rice with apple juice and bring to a boil. Boil for 10 minutes with the pot uncovered, remove from heat, and set aside to cool. Once cool, pat dry with a paper towel.

To build the sushi, knead half of the modeling chocolate until pliable. Roll chocolate into a paper-thin thickness between sheets of waxed paper.

Cut the rolled chocolate into 2½"-wide strips.

Place sticky rice on chocolate strips along the length of the chocolate, leaving a space on one side for the seam.

Arrange your leaves on top of the rice, then your fruit pieces. Roll up tightly, making sure that both sides are stuck together.

Wrap in plastic wrap and freeze for 15 minutes or allow to set in the refrigerator for 2 to 3 hours before cutting. Slice roll into 1" pieces, or any desired thickness. Yield: 4 to 6 servings.

Bev's Bites

If the modeling chocolate is too stiff to roll, rub your hand over the surface, as this will warm up the chocolate and make it easier to manipulate.

If the sushi is sticking to waxed paper and won't release easily, wrap as a long roll in the waxed paper and freeze for about 15 minutes. Unwrap and pinch together seam as necessary.

Don't overthink the measurements when making this. It is intended to be free form and lots of conversation-starting fun!

Chocolate 'Mallow 'Wiches

If you enjoy Moon Pies, you'll love these made-from-scratch sensations. They are well worth all the work!

COOKIES

3½ cups unbleached, all-purpose flour
1¼ cups whole wheat flour
1½ tsp. salt
¾ tsp. baking soda
1¼ cups unsalted butter, room temperature, cut into pieces
⅔ cup confectioners' sugar, sifted
⅓ cup granulated sugar
1 large egg
¼ cup honey
1 tbsp. heavy whipping cream

FILLINGS AND TOPPINGS

1¾ cups warm water, divided
3 .25-oz. envelopes unflavored gelatin
3 cups granulated sugar, divided
1½ cups light corn syrup
6 large egg whites
¼ tsp. cream of tartar
¼ tsp. salt
3 oz. unsweetened chocolate, chopped, melted, and cooled
1 tbsp. vanilla extract
Cornstarch
1½ lbs. milk chocolate, chopped, melted, and cooled slightly
3 oz. white chocolate, chopped, melted, and cooled slightly
3 oz. semisweet chocolate, chopped, melted, and cooled slightly

Bev's Bites

The completed 'wiches can be stored in an airtight container at room temperature for up to 3 days, but who are we kidding? There won't be any left!

For the Cookies: In a large bowl, combine the all-purpose flour and whole wheat flour with the salt and baking soda.

In the large bowl of an electric mixer, beat the butter with the confectioners' sugar and granulated sugar until fluffy. Beat in the egg, followed by the honey and the cream.

Slowly beat the flour mixture into the butter mixture until a dry dough forms. Pat dough into 2 disks, wrap in plastic wrap, and refrigerate until chilled, about 30 minutes.

Heat oven to 350 degrees.

On a lightly floured work surface, roll out 1 disk of dough to a ¼" thickness. Using a 3" round biscuit or cookie cutter, cut out 20 rounds.

Place the rounds on two large cookie sheets and bake for 8 minutes. Turn the cookies over and bake for another 5 to 6 minutes or until golden. Cool cookies on wire racks.

Repeat with the second disk of dough.

For the Fillings and Toppings: In a small saucepan, place ¾ cup of the water and sprinkle the gelatin over the surface. Let stand until softened, about 15 minutes, then cook over medium heat until the gelatin dissolves. Keep warm.

Meanwhile, in a medium saucepan, combine 2½ cups of the sugar with the corn syrup and the remaining 1 cup of water and bring to a boil, stirring until the sugar dissolves. Reduce the heat to medium and simmer until the syrup reaches 240 degrees on a candy thermometer, about 20 minutes. Carefully stir in the warm gelatin.

In the large bowl of an electric mixer, beat the egg whites with the cream of tartar and salt until soft peaks form. With the machine on, gradually add the remaining ½ cup of sugar and beat until stiff peaks form. Beating constantly, slowly pour the hot sugar syrup down the side of the bowl. Beat the marshmallow filling until thick and almost cool, about 5 to 8 minutes.

Lightly oil an 18" x 12" rimmed baking sheet.

When the filling is almost cool, beat in the unsweetened chocolate and the vanilla. Scrape the filling (mixture will be thick) into the pan and smooth the surface with a large offset spatula. Let the marshmallow firm up at room temperature for at least 4 hours or overnight.

To build the 'wiches, arrange half of the cookies, face down, on a work surface.

Dip a 3" round cookie cutter in cornstarch and cut out 20 marshmallow rounds as close together as possible.

Spoon a scant teaspoon of the milk chocolate in the center of each cookie (this will be your "glue") and set a marshmallow round on top. Spoon another scant teaspoon of the milk chocolate in the center of each marshmallow round and cover with the remaining cookies, face up. Refrigerate the cookies until the chocolate hardens, about 10 minutes.

Line two baking sheets with waxed paper. Dip the top of each sandwich into the milk chocolate, letting any excess drip back into the bowl. Set the sandwiches on the baking sheet, chocolate side down. Spread the remaining milk chocolate over the sandwiches to coat them.

Using a small spoon or fork, drizzle the white and semisweet chocolates over the sandwiches and refrigerate until completely set. Yield: 20 'wiches.

Panna Cotta Chocolate Layer Cake Banded with Chocolate

Our tester, Annette, suggests piping a bow using white royal icing on the chocolate band to "wrap up" the entire package. Look for this fun extra in my Cakes to Die For! *cookbook.*

CAKE

- 4 oz. bittersweet chocolate, coarsely chopped
- 3 tbsp. unsweetened cocoa powder
- ½ cup hot brewed coffee
- ½ cup hot water
- 1 cup plus 1 tbsp. unbleached, all-purpose flour
- 1 tsp. baking powder
- ½ tsp. baking soda
- ⅛ tsp. salt
- ⅓ cup vegetable oil
- ½ cup granulated sugar
- ½ cup light brown sugar, firmly packed
- 3 large eggs
- ½ cup sour cream

PANNA COTTA

- ½ cup water
- 5 tsp. unflavored gelatin
- 7½ oz. bittersweet chocolate, coarsely chopped
- 5 oz. milk chocolate, coarsely chopped
- 2½ cups heavy whipping cream
- 2½ cups milk, whole
- ½ cup plus 2 tbsp. granulated sugar
- 1¼ tsp. vanilla extract
- 1¼ vanilla beans, split lengthwise

CHOCOLATE BAND

- 2 16" x 3" strips parchment or waxed paper
- 5 oz. bittersweet chocolate, coarsely chopped

Bev's Bites

Once the panna cotta cake has been layered, it can be covered and frozen for up to 2 weeks. Defrost overnight in the refrigerator before making the chocolate band and wrapping the cake.

For the Cake: Heat oven to 350 degrees. Lightly grease 2 10" x 2½" springform pans.

In a medium bowl, combine chocolate and cocoa powder. Pour coffee and water over chocolate mixture, then whisk until smooth.

In another medium bowl, whisk together the flour, baking powder, baking soda, and salt.

In the large bowl of an electric mixer, beat the oil, granulated sugar, and brown sugar on low speed for 1 minute. Mixture will be crumbly. Add the eggs, one at a time, beating after each addition. Beat in sour cream, then mix in half of the dry ingredients. Beat in entire chocolate mixture, then add remaining dry ingredients and beat on low speed just to blend (batter will be thin). Divide batter between pans. Yes, layers are supposed to be shallow.

Bake about 20 minutes or until a toothpick inserted in the center comes out clean. Cool in pans on wire racks.

For the Panna Cotta: In a small bowl, place water, then sprinkle gelatin over top. Let soften 10 minutes.

Place both chocolates in a large metal bowl.

In a large saucepan, combine the cream, milk, sugar, and vanilla extract. Scrape seeds from the vanilla beans and add both seeds and beans to saucepan. Bring to a boil, stirring until sugar dissolves. Remove from heat; remove vanilla beans. Add gelatin mixture and whisk to dissolve.

Pour cream mixture over chocolates in bowl; whisk until completely melted. Place bowl over a larger bowl of ice water, replacing ice as needed. Stir often until mixture thickens like pudding, about 45 minutes.

Pour half of panna cotta over 1 of the cakes (don't be alarmed if mixture drips down sides of cake). Freeze 45 minutes. Meanwhile, keep remaining panna cotta at room temperature.

Remove pan sides from second cake. Using a large metal spatula, carefully slide cake off pan bottom and place on top of panna cotta in cake pan (as if you were creating a cake-and-panna cotta sandwich). Pour remaining panna cotta over the second cake, filling pan completely. Chill overnight.

For the Chocolate Band: Line a large baking sheet with foil; set aside. Place another large sheet of foil on your work surface and place waxed-paper strips on top of foil, spaced 1" apart.

Place chocolate in a medium bowl set over pan of simmering water; stir until smooth. Pour half of the melted chocolate down the center of each waxed paper strip. Using a small offset spatula, spread chocolate evenly over strips, allowing some of the chocolate to extend beyond edges of the wax paper to make sure that the strips are completely covered.

Using your fingertips, lift strips and place on the foil-lined baking sheet. Chill in the refrigerator until chocolate begins to set *but is still completely flexible,* about 2 to 3 minutes.

To band the cake, cut around pan sides with a slim knife to release cake. Remove sides of pan.

Using your fingertips, lift 1 chocolate band from the foil. Wrap band around cake, waxed paper side out (chocolate should be touching the cake), lining up 1 long edge with the bottom of the cake. The band will be taller than cake. Repeat with the second band on the uncovered side of the cake, arranging so that the ends of the two bands meet.

If bands overlap, trim any excess paper and chocolate. If chocolate is pliable enough, you might be able to press the top edge of the bands toward the cake, forming a slight ruffle. Chill in the refrigerator until chocolate sets, about 5 to 10 minutes. Gently peel off wax paper. Chill cake.

When ready to serve, cut with a long, sharp knife. Yield: 12 to 14 servings.

This recipe takes some time to create, but what better way to wrap up a chocolate cake before serving than with a band of chocolate?

It's a Party!

Geraldine's Devil's Food Cupcakes with White Chocolate Espresso Topping or White Chocolate Lemon Topping

These cupcakes are destined to get that party started.

CUPCAKES

- 1 cup unbleached, all-purpose flour
- ⅓ cup unsweetened cocoa powder, sifted
- ½ tsp. salt
- ½ tsp. baking powder
- ½ tsp. baking soda
- 1 cup granulated sugar
- 2 large eggs
- ½ cup whole milk
- ¼ cup light olive oil or canola oil
- ½ tsp. vanilla extract
- 1 tbsp. espresso powder, dissolved in ½ cup boiling water
- Zest of 1 large orange, finely grated

WHITE CHOCOLATE ESPRESSO TOPPING

- 3 oz. white chocolate, finely chopped
- 1 tbsp. instant espresso powder
- ½ cup plus 1 tbsp. heavy whipping cream
- ⅔ cup confectioners' sugar, sifted

WHITE CHOCOLATE LEMON TOPPING

- ¼ cup plus 2 tbsp. fresh lemon juice
- 1 tbsp. plus 1 tsp. granulated sugar
- ½ vanilla bean, split horizontally
- Lemon zest from ½ a lemon, plus additional for garnish
- 4 oz. white chocolate, finely chopped
- 3 tbsp. heavy whipping cream
- ½ cup unsalted butter, room temperature, cut into pieces
- 1 cup confectioners' sugar, sifted

For the Cupcakes: Heat oven to 325 degrees. Line 16 standard-size cupcake cups with paper liners.

In a medium bowl, whisk together the flour, cocoa powder, salt, baking powder, baking soda, and sugar.

In another medium bowl, combine the eggs, milk, oil, vanilla, and dissolved espresso powder. Whisk by hand until well blended. Add orange zest.

Pour the wet ingredients into the dry ingredients and whisk to combine. Divide batter evenly among the prepared cups, filling them about half full.

Bake until the cupcakes are puffed and feel springy to the touch, 18 to 22 minutes. Let cool completely in the pans on a wire rack. When cool, remove the cupcakes (still in their paper liners) from the cupcake tins. Yield: 16 cupcakes.

For the White Chocolate Espresso Topping: Put the chocolate in a medium bowl.

In a small saucepan, whisk the espresso powder into the cream and bring the mixture to a boil over medium heat. Pour the hot cream over the chocolate and whisk until melted.

Put the bowl of topping in an ice-water bath and stir occasionally until the chocolate cools to 45 degrees, about 20 to 25 minutes.

When cool, whisk in the confectioners' sugar and blend well. Yield: about 1½ cups.

For the White Chocolate Lemon Topping: In a small saucepan, combine the lemon juice and granulated sugar. Scrape the seeds from the vanilla bean into the pan, then add lemon zest. Bring to a boil over medium heat, stirring to dissolve the sugar. Boil until the mixture is reduced by half; it should have the consistency of a syrup. Pour the syrup into a small bowl and refrigerate until it cools to 70 degrees. Remove vanilla bean.

CHOCOLATE DESSERTS TO DIE FOR!

Place chocolate in the large bowl of an electric mixer with the whisk attachment.

In a medium saucepan, bring the cream to a boil over medium heat. Pour the hot cream over the chocolate and beat on high speed until the chocolate melts and the mixture is smooth, about 2 minutes.

Beat in the butter on medium speed, a little at a time, until well blended. Switch the mixer to high and beat until the topping is pale, fluffy, and doubled in volume. Reduce the speed to medium and beat in the cooled lemon syrup and the confectioners' sugar. Scrape down the sides of the bowl. Beat to combine. Yield: about 2 cups.

Put each topping into a pastry bag and pipe a swirl on the top of the cupcakes, half with the espresso topping and half with the lemon. Garnish the lemon cupcakes with freshly grated lemon zest. Store in a cool place until serving.

Chocolate-upon-Chocolate Layer Cake with White Chocolate Curls

The best chocolate cake, hands down!

CAKE

- 3 oz. semisweet chocolate, coarsely chopped
- 1½ cups hot brewed coffee
- 3 cups granulated sugar
- 2½ cups unbleached, all-purpose flour
- 1½ cups unsweetened cocoa powder, not Dutch process
- 2 tsp. baking soda
- ¾ tsp. baking powder
- 1¼ tsp. salt
- 3 large eggs
- ¾ cup light olive oil or canola oil
- 1½ cups buttermilk
- ¾ tsp. vanilla extract

GANACHE FROSTING

- 1 cup heavy whipping cream
- 2 tbsp. granulated sugar
- 2 tbsp. light corn syrup
- 1 lb. semisweet chocolate, finely chopped
- ¼ cup unsalted butter, room temperature, cut into pieces

White chocolate curls, for garnish

Bev's Bites

Cake layers may be made 1 day ahead and kept, wrapped well in plastic wrap, at room temperature.

The finished cake will keep, covered and chilled, for 3 days. Bring cake to room temperature before serving.

For the Cake: Heat oven to 300 degrees. Grease 2 10" deep round cake pans. Line bottoms of the pans with waxed paper; grease the paper.

In a medium bowl, combine chocolate and coffee. Let mixture stand, stirring occasionally, until chocolate is melted and mixture is smooth.

In a large bowl, sift together the sugar, flour, cocoa powder, baking soda, baking powder, and salt.

In the large bowl of an electric mixer, beat eggs until thickened slightly and lemon colored, about 3 to 5 minutes. Slowly add oil, buttermilk, vanilla, and chocolate mixture; beat until well combined. Scrape down the sides of the bowl.

Add sugar mixture and beat on medium speed until well combined, but be careful not to overbeat. Divide batter between pans and bake for 1 hour or until a toothpick inserted in the center comes out clean. Cool layers in pans on wire racks. Carefully remove cakes from pans and waxed paper and cool layers completely.

For the Frosting: In a 2-quart saucepan, bring cream, sugar, and corn syrup to a boil over medium-low heat, whisking until sugar is dissolved. Remove pan from heat and add chocolate, whisking until chocolate is melted. Add butter to saucepan, whisking until smooth.

Transfer frosting to a large bowl and cool, stirring occasionally, until spreadable. If frosting does not firm up, it may be necessary to chill slightly to a spreadable consistency.

Spread frosting between cake layers and over top and sides. Decorate with white chocolate curls when ready to serve. Yield: 12 to 14 servings.

*This is my go-to chocolate layer cake when I want to dress to impress—
it's heaven on a plate!*

Crème fraîche in the batter gives these cupcakes a rich, moist flavor—and the truffle cream topping is, well, to die for!

A Hint-of-Chocolate Cupcakes with Truffle Cream Topping

A hint of chocolate is all that's needed for cupcake bliss.

CUPCAKES

1½ cups unbleached, all-purpose flour
1 tsp. baking powder
½ tsp. baking soda
¼ tsp. salt
3 oz. bittersweet chocolate, finely grated
8 oz. crème fraîche, room temperature
3 large eggs, room temperature
1 tsp. vanilla extract
6 tbsp. unsalted butter, room temperature
¾ cup granulated sugar

TRUFFLE CREAM TOPPING

8 oz. semisweet chocolate, coarsely chopped
⅔ cup heavy whipping cream
⅔ cup plus 2 tbsp. confectioners' sugar, sifted
4 tbsp. unsalted butter, room temperature
1 tbsp. vanilla extract

For the Cupcakes: Heat oven to 325 degrees. Line 18 standard cupcake cups with paper liners.

In a medium bowl, whisk together the flour, baking powder, baking soda, salt, and chocolate.

In another medium bowl, combine the crème fraîche, eggs, and vanilla and whisk until well combined.

In the large bowl of an electric mixer, beat the butter on medium speed until creamy. Scrape down the sides of the bowl. Add the sugar and beat until light and fluffy. On low speed, alternate adding the dry ingredients with the wet ingredients in three batches. Divide the batter evenly among the cupcake cups, filling them ½ to ⅔ full.

Bake until the cupcakes are puffed, lightly browned, slightly cracked on top and a toothpick inserted in the center comes out clean, about 20 to 25 minutes. Let cool completely in pan on a wire rack. When cool, remove the cupcakes (still in their papers) from the cupcake pans.

For the Truffle Cream Topping: Put the chocolate in a medium bowl.

In a small saucepan, combine the cream and confectioners' sugar and bring to a simmer over medium heat. Cook at a simmer for 1 minute; remove saucepan from heat.

Pour the hot cream mixture over the chocolate. Whisk the mixture by hand until the chocolate melts, then whisk in the butter and vanilla until smooth.

Cover with plastic wrap so that the plastic touches the surface. Refrigerate for 40 minutes.

Place chocolate cream mixture in the large bowl of an electric mixer with the whisk attachment. Beat on high speed until the mixture is light and fluffy. Put the topping in a pastry bag and pipe a swirl on the top center of each cupcake, distributing the topping evenly among them. Store in a cool place until serving. Yield: 18 cupcakes.

It's a Party!

Chicago-Style Deep-Dish Dessert Pizza

Everyone loves pizza (and pizza parties), and this dessert version is sure to fit the bill.

PIZZA CRUST

- 3 cups unbleached, all-purpose flour
- 1 tsp. baking powder
- ½ tsp. salt
- 4 tbsp. granulated sugar
- 2 large egg yolks
- 1 tsp. vanilla extract
- 4½ oz. white chocolate, melted
- 1½ cups unsalted butter, cold, cut into small pieces

TOPPINGS

- 1 cup heavy whipping cream
- ¼ cup light brown sugar, firmly packed
- 1 cup dried cranberries, lightly snipped
- 1 cup dried tart cherries, lightly snipped
- 4 oz. dried apricots, finely diced
- 1 cup coarsely chopped pecans, lightly toasted
- 4½ oz. bittersweet chocolate, coarsely chopped
- 4 oz. white chocolate, coarsely chopped

For the Pizza Crust: Heat oven to 375 degrees. Lightly grease a 9" springform pan.

In a medium bowl, whisk together the flour, baking powder, and salt. Set aside.

In a medium bowl, whisk together the sugar, egg yolks, and vanilla until combined and the sugar is dissolved. Add the white chocolate and whisk to combine. Set aside.

In the large bowl of an electric mixer, mix the dry ingredients with the butter on low speed until the butter is blended and the mixture resembles coarse crumbs. Add the wet ingredients and blend on low just until a loose dough forms.

Transfer the dough to a clean, dry work surface, and knead it gently to form a smooth dough.

Place the dough in the prepared pan. Use your clean fingertips to press the dough first into the bottom and then ¾ of the way up the sides of the pan. Bake for 14 minutes, then remove from oven and allow to cool at room temperature on a wire rack.

For the Toppings: In a 3-quart saucepan, heat the cream and brown sugar over medium heat, stirring to dissolve the sugar. Bring to a boil, then allow to simmer until slightly thickened. Remove saucepan from the heat and add the dried fruits and pecans, stirring gently to combine.

Gently spoon the fruit and nut mixture evenly over the crust. Sprinkle the bittersweet chocolate pieces evenly over the fruit and nut mixture.

Place the pan on the oven's center rack and bake for 25 to 30 minutes or until the crust is lightly browned around the edges. Remove from the oven and allow to cool on a wire rack for 45 minutes.

Melt the white chocolate and, using a fork or a small spoon, drizzle in a zigzag pattern over the entire surface of the pizza. Allow the chocolate to become firm at room temperature before serving. To serve, remove the pizza from the pan and cut with a serrated knife. Yield: 10 to 14 servings.

Chicago-style deep-dish pizza has never been such a sweet treat.

It's a Party!

Chocolate Fettuccine with Whipped Cream and Fudge Sauce

This dish is great fun to make ahead in stages and then serve as a spectacularly simple dessert for a dinner party.

3 large eggs
⅛ tsp. salt
1 cup milk, whole or 2%
1 cup *less* 2 level tbsp. unbleached, all-purpose flour
2 tbsp. clarified butter, melted, plus additional for pan
2 tbsp. unsweetened cocoa powder, sifted
1 tbsp. vanilla extract
1 tbsp. granulated sugar
1 cup heavy whipping cream
Fudge sauce, for serving

Bev's Bites

Clarifying butter is a process of melting unsalted butter in a heavy pan over low heat, keeping it from browning, and skimming off the white froth that rises to the top with a spoon. The clean yellow "clarified" liquid butter should be kept and the white curd-like dregs discarded. Clarified butter allows foods to be cooked at a higher temperature and for a longer time without the butter blackening and becoming acrid.

Allowing the batter to rest is important—it enables the flour to expand and absorb the liquid. A batter that has rested will work much better than one that's freshly made.

When making and stacking the crêpes, put a piece of waxed paper between each cooked crêpe to prevent them from sticking together.

In a blender or food processor, combine eggs, salt, milk, flour, butter, cocoa powder, vanilla, and sugar. Process to combine, stopping and scraping down the sides as needed, until smooth and well mixed.

Pour mixture into a bowl and cover with plastic wrap. Let batter rest at room temperature for 2 to 3 hours or up to 12 hours in the refrigerator.

Brush the inside of a crêpe or 7" omelet pan with clarified butter. Heat the pan over medium-high heat. Pour ¼ cup of the batter into the hot pan, swirling quickly to cover the bottom.

Cook on one side until the edges are lightly browned. Flip the crêpe (using a metal spatula and your clean fingers) and cook for 15 additional seconds. Repeat until all batter is used. Let cool. Yield: about 12 crêpes.

Whip heavy whipping cream to soft peaks; set aside.

Cut each crêpe into long strands about ¼" wide with a very sharp knife. Separate the strands, place in a large pasta bowl, and toss lightly with your fingers so that they resemble fettuccine noodles.

Spoon the whipped cream into the center of the pasta bowl. Toss the "fettuccine" with the whipped cream and serve with fudge sauce. Yield: 4 to 6 servings.

Bold Chocolate Fudge Cake
Temptingly simple.

12 oz. semisweet chocolate, coarsely chopped
5 tbsp. espresso or double strength brewed dark roast coffee
2 cups granulated sugar
1 cup unsalted butter, room temperature, cut into pieces
6 large eggs, separated, room temperature
1 cup unbleached, all-purpose flour
Confectioners' sugar, for garnish

Heat oven to 350 degrees. Lightly grease and flour a 9" springform pan.

In top of a double boiler over hot—not simmering—water, melt together the chocolate and espresso, stirring occasionally until smooth. Scrape chocolate mixture into a large bowl and allow to cool for 10 to 15 minutes or until just slightly warm to the touch.

In a large bowl, beat the sugar and butter with a handheld mixer at medium-high speed until light and fluffy. Add the eggs yolks one at a time, beating well after each addition. Beat in the flour.

In the large bowl of an electric mixer, beat egg whites at medium-high speed until they form stiff, shiny peaks. Fold ¼ of the egg whites into the chocolate mixture to lighten it, then fold in remaining egg whites. Fold in the sugar mixture.

Gently scrape batter into prepared pan and bake for 60 to 70 minutes or until the top is crusty and lightly cracked and the middle is still slightly moist. Remove cake from oven to a wire rack, gently run a knife around the inside edge of the cake to loosen, and allow to cool completely in the pan.

When ready to serve, remove sides of springform pan and transfer cake to a serving plate. Sprinkle with confectioners' sugar. Yield: 8 to 10 servings.

Shaken or Stirred? Chocolatini

An artfully mixed chocolate Martini—shaken or stirred—is a thing of beauty. This is a delightfully naughty recipe.

Chocolate-flavored vodka, unsweetened, or 750 ml. *less* 8 oz. high-quality, plain vodka
1 cup cocoa nibs, preferably fresh, or according to taste
Favorite garnishes (for example, chocolate shavings, chocolate syrup, or cocoa powder)

Bev's Bites

There are several ways to make a Chocolatini that are not sweet. Choose the method that suits your palate and your patience.

In addition to the traditional chocolate garnishes, other delicious selections might include chocolate-covered coffee beans or lemon- or orange-peel twists.

To make your own chocolate-flavored vodka, add cocoa nibs to vodka. Cap the bottle and infuse for three days, shaking the bottle once daily. After three days, test the vodka. If you want more chocolate flavor, let the vodka infuse for a few more days, shaking the bottle once daily.

When the infused vodka attains a flavor you like, strain the vodka through several layers of cheesecloth to remove the nibs and any sediment. Viola!

Now, to make that chocolatini: Fill a cocktail shaker with ice and add the chocolate infused vodka. Shake and strain into a cocktail glass garnished with your choice of garnish. Cheers!

Left: *Vodka with cocoa nibs, ready for steeping.*
Right: *Voilà! Chocolate-infused vodka.*

Chocolate Blackout Cookies

Add these eyes-wide-open cookies to your collection.

- 3 oz. unsweetened chocolate, coarsely chopped
- 18 oz. semisweet chocolate, coarsely chopped, divided
- ½ cup plus 1 tbsp. unsalted butter, room temperature
- 3 large eggs
- 1 cup plus 2 tbsp. granulated sugar
- 1 tbsp. instant espresso powder
- 1 tbsp. vanilla extract
- 6 tbsp. unbleached, all-purpose flour, sifted
- ½ tsp. baking powder
- ¾ tsp. salt
- 1½ cups walnut pieces, lightly toasted
- 1½ cups pecan pieces, lightly toasted

Heat oven to 325 degrees.

In a double boiler or metal bowl set over a pan of barely simmering water, melt the unsweetened chocolate, 9 oz. of the semisweet chocolate, and butter, stirring occasionally. When melted, remove top of double boiler or bowl from heat.

In the large bowl of an electric mixer, beat eggs with sugar until light and fluffy. Add espresso powder, vanilla, and chocolate mixture, beating until smooth.

In a small bowl, whisk together the flour, baking powder, and salt and add to the chocolate mixture, beating just until combined. Stir in remaining 9 oz. semisweet chocolate and nuts until well combined.

With a ½-cup measure, scoop out cookie dough onto ungreased cookie sheets, arranging them 3" apart. Bake on racks in the middle of the oven for 22 to 25 minutes or until tops begin to crack but are not yet dry (do not over bake). Cool cookies on wire rack. Yield: 1 dozen large cookies.

Why wait for a blackout? Be bold—eat these with all the lights on!

It's a Party!

Fondue: Pick Your Fave!

Fondue is a great party food. It's simple to make, fun to eat, and makes for a memorable evening. Grab a skewer and take a dip with me!

MOCHA FONDUE

¾ cup heavy whipping cream
1 lb. semisweet chocolate, finely chopped
¼ cup coffee liqueur

Bev's Bites

All of these fondues can be made either the traditional stovetop way or quickly and easily in the Vitamix blender.

CHOCOLATE AND COCONUT CREAM FONDUE

15 oz. sweetened cream of coconut
12 oz. bittersweet chocolate, finely chopped
¼ cup heavy whipping cream
¼ tsp. coconut extract

For the Mocha Fondue: In a medium saucepan, bring the cream to a boil. Remove from heat and add chocolate, stirring until smooth. Stir in liqueur. Spoon into fondue pot and keep warm over low heat. Serve with desired dippers. Yield: 10 to 12 servings.

In the Vitamix container, place the cream and chocolate. Secure lid and select Variable 1. Slowly increase speed to Variable 10, then High, using tamper to press chocolate into blades. Blend for about 3 minutes or until chocolate is melted and mixture is hot. Spoon into fondue pot and stir in liqueur. Keep warm over low heat. Serve with desired dippers. Yield: 10 to 12 servings.

Dipper suggestions: biscotti pieces, strawberries, pineapple chunks, banana chunks.

For the Chocolate and Coconut Cream Fondue: In a medium saucepan, combine the cream of coconut and chocolate. Stir mixture over very low heat until chocolate melts and mixture is smooth. Stir in heavy whipping cream and coconut extract. Spoon into fondue pot and keep warm over low heat. Serve with desired dippers. Yield: 8 servings.

In the Vitamix container, place the cream of coconut, chocolate, heavy whipping cream, and coconut extract. Secure lid and select Variable 1. Slowly increase speed to Variable 10, then High, using tamper to press ingredients into blades. Blend for about 3 minutes or until chocolate is melted and mixture is hot. Spoon into fondue pot and keep warm over low heat. Serve with desired dippers. Yield: 8 servings.

Dipper suggestions: mango chunks, pineapple chunks, banana chunks, tangerine or clementine segments.

PEANUT BUTTER AND CHOCOLATE FONDUE

⅓ cup milk, whole or 2%
12 oz. milk chocolate, finely chopped
2 tbsp. peanut butter

Bev's Bites
If the peanut butter and chocolate mixture gets too thick, add additional milk to thin as desired.

For the Peanut Butter and Chocolate Fondue: In a medium saucepan over low heat, combine the milk and chocolate. Heat, stirring constantly, until chocolate is melted and smooth. Stir in peanut butter. Heat through. Spoon into fondue pot and keep warm over low heat. Serve with desired dippers. Yield: 6 servings.

In the Vitamix container, place the milk, chocolate, and peanut butter. Secure lid and select Variable 1. Slowly increase speed to Variable 10, then High, using tamper to press chocolate into blades. Blend for about 3 minutes or until chocolate is melted and mixture is hot. Spoon into fondue pot and keep warm over low heat. Serve with desired dippers. Yield: 6 servings.

Dipper suggestions: cake cubes, marshmallows, strawberries, pretzels.

It's a Party!

Downsized Turtle Pecan Pie

What fun to serve a scaled, model dessert for two!

TURTLE PECAN PIE

- ½ cup unbleached, all-purpose flour
- ¼ cup plus 4 tsp. granulated sugar, divided
- 3 tbsp. unsalted butter, cut into pieces
- 1 tsp. water
- 1 large egg
- ¼ cup light corn syrup
- 1 tsp. vanilla extract
- 3 tbsp. pecan pieces
- 3 tbsp. semisweet chocolate, coarsely chopped

CARAMEL SAUCE

- 1 tbsp. unsalted butter
- 5 tbsp. granulated sugar
- ¼ cup heavy whipping cream

Bev's Bites

If making Caramel Sauce ahead, cover and chill up to 1 week, reheating before using.

For the Pie: Mix flour with 4 tsp. of the sugar and butter to make coarse crumbs. Stir in water. Press dough into a disk, then press it over bottom and ¾" up sides of a lightly greased 6" cake or tart pan with a removable bottom. Prick lightly with a fork. Freeze 30 minutes.

Heat oven to 375 degrees.

Bake crust about 15 to 20 minutes or just until crust is a light golden brown. Remove from oven. Lower oven temperature to 350 degrees.

In a medium bowl, blend remaining ¼ cup sugar, egg, corn syrup, vanilla, pecans, and chocolate. Pour into warm crust and bake until filing is set when pan is gently shaken, about 25 to 30 minutes. Cool on a wire rack for 30 minutes before serving. Accompany with warm Caramel Sauce. Yield: 3 or 4 servings.

For the Caramel Sauce: In a 1½-quart saucepan, combine the butter and sugar over medium-high heat. Shake pan frequently to mix until sugar is melted and amber in color; watch carefully so sugar doesn't burn. Remove saucepan from heat and add cream. (Caution: mixture will sputter!) Stir until caramel is smoothly mixed with cream. Yield: about 5 tbsp.

Chocolate Peanut Butter Ice Cream Pie with Chocolate-Cookie Crust

Always a favorite—especially with a drizzle of Fudge Sauce.

CHOCOLATE-COOKIE CRUST

1 cup chocolate cookies, finely ground
2 tbsp. granulated sugar
3 to 4 tbsp. unsalted butter, melted

FILLING

2 cups chocolate ice cream, softened slightly
4 cups vanilla ice cream, softened slightly
⅓ cup peanut butter
2 tbsp. salted peanuts, chopped

Fudge sauce, for serving

For the Crust: Heat oven to 350 degrees.

In a medium bowl, mix the cookie crumbs and sugar with a fork until blended. Drizzle the melted butter over the crumbs and mix with a fork until the crumbs are evenly moistened.

Place the crumbs in a 9" or 10" pie pan and use your clean hands to spread the crumbs so that they coat the bottom of the pan and start to climb the sides. Use your fingers to pinch and press some of the crumbs around the inside edge of the pan to cover the sides evenly. Bake for 6 to 8 minutes or until fragrant. Cool completely on a wire rack.

For the Filling: Spread softened chocolate ice cream over bottom of crust. Freeze until firm, at least 30 minutes.

In the large bowl of an electric mixer, combine vanilla ice cream and peanut butter. Beat at low speed until peanut butter is evenly distributed, scraping down the sides of the bowl often. Freeze until mixture holds soft mounds when scooped, about 30 to 45 minutes.

Spoon peanut butter mixture over chocolate ice cream layer. Spread to edges of crust, mounding slightly higher in center. Sprinkle with chopped peanuts. Freeze 4 to 5 hours or until firm.

When ready to serve, let stand at room temperature 5 minutes before serving. Drizzle with fudge sauce. Yield: 8 servings.

It's a Party!

Chocolate Sorbet

So few ingredients, such great flavors.

4 oz. bittersweet chocolate, finely chopped
½ cup unsweetened cocoa powder, sifted
1 tbsp. espresso powder
2 cups water
1¼ cups granulated sugar

In a medium bowl, combine the chocolate, cocoa powder, and espresso powder.

In a medium saucepan, combine the water and sugar and cook over medium heat, stirring occasionally, until sugar dissolves. Bring syrup to a boil, reduce heat, and simmer for 2 to 3 minutes. Pour sugar syrup over chocolate mixture and let stand for 1 minute.

Whisk until smooth and allow to cool to room temperature, stirring occasionally. Cover sorbet base and refrigerate until well chilled, 2 to 3 hours.

Whisk chilled sorbet base until smooth. Pour mixture into an ice cream maker and freeze according to manufacturer's instructions, or alternatively, pour into popsicle molds and freeze.

If using an ice cream maker: When cycle is complete, pack into a container and freeze for 2 to 3 hours or overnight. Yield: 6 servings.

Pure chocolate flavor, frozen and on a stick!

Bread and Chocolate: A Little Dessert Bruschetta

As this recipe shows, the very best ingredients and the simplest preparations yield spectacular results.

- 1 baguette, cut diagonally into at least 25 ½" slices
- 6 to 8 tbsp. unsalted butter, melted
- ¾ cup bittersweet chocolate, finely grated
- ¼ cup semisweet chocolate, coarsely grated
- ¾ cup milk chocolate, finely grated

Bev's Bites

Depending on the diameter of your baguette, you may want to cut each slice in half. The end result should be slender "fingers" of bread.

Heat oven to 350 degrees.

Brush butter lightly on one side of the baguette slices; put on foil lined baking sheets and toast in the oven just until crispy, 5 to 7 minutes. Remove from oven and let cool on a wire rack.

In a medium bowl, combine the bittersweet, semisweet, and milk chocolates. Sprinkle mixture generously on top of cooled bread slices. Return baking sheet to the oven to soften and warm the chocolate mixture, about 10 to 12 additional minutes. Serve immediately. Yield: more than 12 servings.

Sour Cream Chocolate Layer Cake with Whipped Chocolate Cream Frosting or Milk Chocolate Frosting

The frosting variations match the richness and love found in this dark and not-too-sweet chocolate layer cake.

CAKE

- 1 cup hot, brewed, double-strength dark-roast coffee
- ½ cup sour cream, room temperature
- ½ cup vegetable oil
- 2 cups granulated sugar
- 1¾ cups unbleached, all-purpose flour
- ¾ tsp. baking soda
- ½ tsp. salt
- 2 large eggs
- 4 oz. unsweetened chocolate, melted

WHIPPED CHOCOLATE CREAM FROSTING

- ½ cup semisweet chocolate, coarsely chopped
- ½ cup heavy whipping cream
- 1½ cups confectioners' sugar, sifted
- ½ cup unsalted butter, room temperature, cut into pieces
- ½ tsp. vanilla extract

MILK CHOCOLATE FROSTING

- 2 cups milk chocolate, coarsely chopped
- 6 tbsp. unsalted butter, room temperature, cut into pieces
- ½ tsp. salt
- 2½ cups confectioners' sugar, sifted
- ¼ to ⅓ cup milk
- 1 tsp. vanilla extract

For the Cake: Heat oven to 345 degrees. Lightly grease 2 8" round cake pans, then line with parchment paper circles.

In a large mixing bowl, whisk together the hot coffee, sour cream, and vegetable oil.

In the large bowl of an electric mixer, combine the sugar, flour, baking soda, and salt and beat on low speed while adding the coffee mixture in a steady stream. Scrape down the sides of the bowl.

Add the eggs, one at a time, beating well after each addition. Scrape down the sides of the bowl. Add the chocolate and mix until the batter is well blended. Divide evenly between the prepared pans and bake until the cake springs back to the touch and a toothpick inserted in the center comes out dry, 35 to 37 minutes.

Cool the layers in the pan on a wire rack for 15 minutes, then invert onto racks, remove parchment paper, and reinvert so the cakes are right side up. Allow to cool completely. Frost cake and allow to set in the refrigerator before serving. Yield: 12 to 14 servings once frosted.

For the Whipped Chocolate Cream Frosting: Combine in a double boiler over hot (not boiling) water the chocolate and the cream. Stir until chocolate is melted and mixture is smooth. Chill thoroughly.

In the large bowl of an electric mixer, beat together the confectioners' sugar, butter, and vanilla. Gradually add chocolate mixture. Beat until stiff. Frost cake. Yield: about 2⅓ cups frosting.

For the Milk Chocolate Frosting: Combine in a double boiler over hot (not boiling) water the chocolate, butter, and salt. Stir until chocolate is melted and mixture is smooth. Remove from heat and transfer to the large bowl of an electric mixer.

Gradually beat in the confectioners' sugar alternately with the milk until the mixture reaches a desired spreading consistency. Scrape down the sides of the bowl, then beat in vanilla. Frost cake. Yield: about 2½ cups frosting.

It's a Party!

Crisp, flaky, chocolate goodness in every appetizer bite!

Mini Chocolate Turnovers

Dessert as an appetizer? When it comes to chocolate, anything goes . . .

2 large eggs, divided
2 tbsp. low-fat Greek yogurt, well drained
⅓ cup plus 1 tbsp. granulated sugar, divided
2 tsp. vanilla
1 tbsp. unbleached, all-purpose flour
1 tbsp. unsweetened cocoa powder, sifted
⅓ cup chopped pistachios, toasted
2 oz. semisweet chocolate, finely chopped
1 tbsp. water
1 17.3-oz. package (2 sheets) frozen puff pastry, thawed
Confectioners' sugar, sifted, for sprinkling

Heat oven to 400 degrees.

Line two baking sheets with parchment paper or silicone liners. Set aside.

In a medium bowl, combine one of the eggs, yogurt, ⅓ cup of the granulated sugar, and vanilla. Stir in the flour and cocoa powder until combined, then stir in pistachios and chocolate.

In a small bowl, combine the remaining egg and water. Set aside.

On a lightly floured surface, unfold each sheet of puff pastry. Roll each pastry into a 12" square. Using a sharp knife or pizza cutter, cut each pastry sheet into 9 4" squares.

Spoon about 1 teaspoon of the chocolate mixture into the center of each square. Brush edges of pastry with egg-water mixture. Fold each square in half diagonally to form a triangle; press edges with a fork to seal.

Place turnovers on the prepared baking sheets.

Brush tops with egg-water mixture and sprinkle with remaining 1 tbsp. sugar. Bake about 15 to 20 minutes or until golden. Before serving, sprinkle turnovers with confectioners' sugar. Serve warm. Yield: 18 appetizer turnovers.

Jumbo Double-Fudge Brownie Muffins

Why go small when only jumbo will do?

- 3 oz. unsweetened chocolate, coarsely chopped
- 3 oz. semisweet chocolate, coarsely chopped
- 6 tbsp. unsalted butter, room temperature
- 1½ cups unbleached, all-purpose flour
- 1 tsp. baking powder
- ½ tsp. baking soda
- ¼ tsp. salt
- 2 large eggs
- ½ cup granulated sugar
- ½ cup milk
- 1 tsp. vanilla
- 1 cup semisweet chocolate chips
- ½ cup pine nuts, coarsely chopped and lightly toasted

Heat oven to 350 degrees. Line 6 to 8 jumbo muffin cups with paper baking cups and set aside.

Melt the unsweetened chocolate, semisweet chocolate, and butter in a medium saucepan, stirring occasionally until smooth. Set aside and cool for 15 minutes.

In a large bowl, whisk together the flour, baking powder, baking soda, and salt.

In a medium bowl, whisk together the eggs, sugar, milk, and vanilla. Add the chocolate-butter mixture, whisking until blended.

With a rubber spatula, fold the egg mixture into the dry ingredients, folding only until dry ingredients are moistened. Gently stir in chocolate chips and pine nuts.

Fill the muffin cups ¾ full.

Bake for 18 to 20 minutes or until springy to the touch. Cool in the pan on a wire rack for 5 minutes. Remove and enjoy, or cool completely. Yield: 6 to 8 jumbo muffins (or up to 16 regular size).

Shareable muffins that are easily pried apart—lots of crumbs and fun for all.

Chocolate Chip Cookie Dough Cheesecake

For all of you who love chocolate chip cookie dough, this is the perfect dessert surprise—a simplified cookie dough batter in a smooth cheesecake.

CRUST

- 1½ cups chocolate wafers, finely crushed
- 1 cup granulated sugar
- ¼ cup plus 1 tbsp. unsalted butter, melted

COOKIE DOUGH

- ¼ cup unsalted butter, room temperature
- ¼ cup light brown sugar, firmly packed
- ¼ cup granulated sugar
- 2 tbsp. water
- 1 tsp. vanilla extract
- ½ cup unbleached, all-purpose flour
- 1 cup semisweet chocolate chips

CHEESECAKE FILLING

- 16 oz. cream cheese, room temperature, cut into pieces
- 1 cup sour cream
- 3 large eggs
- 1 tsp. vanilla extract

For the Crust: Heat oven to 350 degrees.

In a medium bowl, mix together the crushed wafers, sugar, and melted butter. Press over bottom and ½" up sides of a 9" springform pan. Bake for 8 minutes. Cool on a wire rack. Leave oven on.

For the Cookie Dough: In the large bowl of an electric mixer, beat together the butter, brown sugar, and granulated sugar until light and fluffy. Scrape down the sides and bottom of the bowl. Stir in the water and vanilla until combined.

Beat in the flour until blended. Stir in the chocolate chips. Set aside.

For the Cheesecake Filling: In the large bowl of an electric mixer, beat the cream cheese until creamy. With mixer on medium speed, add the sour cream, eggs, and vanilla until light and well blended. Scrape down the sides of the bowl. Spread batter onto prepared crust.

Drop cookie dough over entire surface of cheesecake batter in 2 tbsp. increments. Push cookie dough beneath the surface of the cheesecake filling. Bake for 40 minutes or until center appears nearly set. (Center will still jiggle but not be liquidy.) Cool in pan on a wire rack. Cover loosely with wax paper and refrigerate cheesecake overnight.

When ready to serve, run a knife around the inside edge of the pan and carefully remove sides. Yield: 12 to 14 servings.

From Bev Shaffer, *Cakes to Die For!* (Gretna, LA: Pelican, 2010). Reprinted by permission of the publisher.

CHOCOLATE GIFTS

Kids beware—the adults might not share these The Kid in All Adults Marshmallow Truffles.

Your friends know that you love chocolate . . . why not create some fabulous gifts from this creative collection of offerings. Gift cards? Forget it! They'll want your homemade chocolate creations instead, wrapped with a bow and ready to devour.

Holiday Chocolate Drops

Green pistachio nuts and dark red dried cranberries make these drop cookies into holiday delights.

1 cup unsalted butter, room temperature
¾ cup granulated sugar
¾ cup light brown sugar, firmly packed
3½ oz. unsweetened chocolate, melted
2 large eggs
1 tsp. vanilla extract
2 cups unbleached, all-purpose flour
1 tsp. baking soda
1 cup pistachio nuts, toasted and chopped
1 cup dried cranberries, snipped

CITRUS DRIZZLE

1½ cups confectioners' sugar, sifted
2 to 3 tbsp. fresh orange juice, without pulp

Heat oven to 350 degrees.

In the large bowl of an electric mixer, combine the butter, granulated sugar, and brown sugar and beat at medium speed until light and fluffy. Scrape down the sides of the bowl. Add chocolate, eggs, and vanilla and continue beating until well mixed.

Reduce speed to low. Add flour and baking soda and beat until well mixed. Stir in pistachio nuts and cranberries by hand.

Drop dough by rounded teaspoonful 2" apart onto ungreased cookie sheets. Bake for 10 to 14 minutes or until cookies are set. Cool completely on a wire rack. Yield: 4½ dozen cookies.

For the Citrus Drizzle: In a small bowl, whisk together the confectioners' sugar and orange juice until it reaches a desired drizzling consistency. Drizzle over cooled cookies. Yield: about 1 cup.

Fudgy Brownie Mix

What fun to keep this brownie mix in your cupboards! It's always ready as a go-to gift for a timid baker or an aspiring foodie.

2 cups granulated sugar
1 cup unsweetened cocoa powder, not Dutch process
1 cup unbleached, all-purpose flour
1 cup pecans, chopped
1 cup semisweet chocolate chips

Layer all ingredients in any order in a 1½- to 2-quart decorative jar.

Attach the following recipe:

DOUBLE FUDGE BROWNIES

1 cup unsalted butter, room temperature, cut into pieces
4 large eggs
1 container Fudgy Brownie Mix

Heat oven to 325 degrees. Grease a 13" x 9" baking pan.

In the large bowl of an electric mixer, cream the butter. Scrape down the sides of the bowl. Add eggs, one at a time, beating well after each addition.

Add the Fudgy Brownie Mix and beat the mixture until well blended. Spread into the prepared pan and bake for 35 to 45 minutes or until a toothpick inserted in the center comes out with a few moist crumbs. Yield: 18 to 24 brownies.

Gifting from your kitchen never tasted so good! Give some chocolate love today.

Chewy chocolate delights—cut them and stick them on lollipop sticks or wrap them! Yours to enjoy.

Chocolate Caramels

Chewy chocolate delights.

1 cup unsalted butter, cut into pieces
2¼ cups light brown sugar, firmly packed
1 cup light corn syrup
14 oz. sweetened condensed milk
2 oz. unsweetened chocolate, coarsely chopped
1½ tsp. vanilla extract

Bev's Bites

A cleaver or a thin-bladed knife works well for cutting the caramels. If making rounds for caramel pops, a 2" cookie or biscuit cutter works well.

Lightly butter a foil-lined 9" square pan.

In a large saucepan, melt butter. Add the brown sugar and mix well. Stir in the corn syrup. Cook over medium-low heat until sugar dissolves and mixture is well blended.

Stir in the sweetened condensed milk and cook over medium heat, stirring constantly, until mixture reaches 230 degrees on a candy thermometer, about 30 minutes or more.

Stir in the chocolate and continue cooking until mixture reaches the soft-ball stage (240 degrees), about 20 minutes or more. Remove saucepan from heat and stir in vanilla. Pour hot mixture into prepared pan and allow to cool.

Refrigerate several hours or until candy has completely set. Remove from pan and cut as desired. Wrap individual pieces in waxed paper and store, well covered, in refrigerator. Yield: About 44 small pieces.

Triple Chocolate Biscotti

Biscotti freeze beautifully, so don't worry about this collection being wasted.

- ⅓ cup plus 1 tbsp. unsalted butter, room temperature
- ⅔ cup granulated sugar
- ¼ cup unsweetened Dutch process cocoa powder, sifted
- 2 tsp. baking powder
- 2 large eggs
- 1¾ cups unbleached, all-purpose flour
- 4 oz. white chocolate, coarsely chopped
- 3 oz. bittersweet chocolate, coarsely chopped

Heat oven to 375 degrees.

In the large bowl of an electric mixer, beat butter until softened. Add the sugar, cocoa powder, and baking powder, and beat until well blended. Scrape down the sides of the bowl.

Beat in the eggs until blended, then add the flour. Stir in the white and bittersweet chocolate pieces.

Divide dough in half and shape each portion into an 8-10" log. Place logs about 4" apart on a parchment paper-lined cookie sheet. Flatten each log slightly to about 2" wide.

Bake for 22 minutes. Cool on the cookie sheet on a wire rack for 30 minutes. On a cutting board, cut each log diagonally into ½"-thick slices using a serrated knife. Lay slices, cut side down, on an ungreased cookie sheet.

Reduce oven to 325 degrees. Bake slices for 8 minutes, turn slices over, then bake for an additional 7 to 9 minutes or just until biscotti are dry and crisp. Cool thoroughly on a wire rack. Yield: 2 dozen biscotti.

From Bev and John Shaffer, *No Reservations Required* (Wooster, OH: Wooster Book Company, 2003). Reprinted by permission of the publisher.

*The crunch of these Triple Chocolate Biscotti make him particularly hard-headed—
but don't worry, he'll still share.*

Crisp Chocolate Biscotti

If you aren't a walnut fan, substitute another nut . . . pistachio perhaps?

- 1¾ cups plus 2 tbsp. unbleached, all-purpose flour
- ⅔ cup unsweetened Dutch process cocoa powder, sifted
- 2 tsp. baking powder
- Pinch of salt
- 1¼ cups granulated sugar
- 1½ cups walnuts, coarsely chopped and lightly toasted
- 4 large eggs
- 1 tsp. vanilla extract

Heat oven to 325 degrees. Line a jellyroll pan with either parchment paper or a silicone mat.

In a medium bowl, sift together the flour, cocoa powder, baking powder, and salt. Stir in granulated sugar and nuts.

In a small bowl, whisk together the eggs and vanilla. Stir egg mixture into the flour mixture to form a dough.

On a lightly floured surface, press dough together without overworking. Divide dough in half and shape each half into a log slightly smaller than the length of a jellyroll pan.

Place each log on the prepared pan and flatten slightly (dough will be sticky). Bake for 30 minutes or until well risen and firm. Cool logs in the pan on a wire rack.

Cut into ½"-thick slices with a serrated knife. Replace, cut side down, on the same lined baking pans and bake again for 15 to 20 minutes or just until dry and crisp. Yield: 2½ dozen biscotti.

Biscotti, ready and waiting for dunking. Got espresso, anyone?

Hard and crunchy, this Chocolate-Covered Almond Butter Crunch is always a welcome gift.

Chocolate-Covered Almond Butter Crunch

Giving this as a gift? Don't forget to save some for yourself.

3½ cups whole almonds, toasted, divided
1½ cups granulated sugar
½ cup light corn syrup
¼ cup water
2 tsp. unsalted butter
1 tsp. baking soda
½ tsp. salt
12 oz. bittersweet chocolate, coarsely chopped

Line a baking sheet with parchment paper or a silicone liner.

In a food processor, pulse 2 cups of the almonds 4 to 5 times until the nuts are coarsely chopped. Scrape onto a large plate and set aside.

In a 3-quart saucepan, combine the sugar, corn syrup, and water. Attach a candy thermometer to the side of the pan, making sure that the end doesn't touch the bottom of the pan. Cook the mixture on medium-high heat, occasionally brushing down the sides of the pan with a pastry brush dipped in water to prevent sugar crystals from forming. Cook until the mixture reaches 310 degrees. Using a wooden spoon, stir in the remaining 1½ cups of almonds, then remove the saucepan from the heat.

Quickly add the butter, baking soda, and salt. The baking soda will make the mixture bubble and harden very quickly. Pour the mixture onto the lined baking sheet and spread it quickly and as thinly as possible. Allow to cool completely.

Break the brittle into small pieces with your hands.

Line another baking sheet with parchment paper or a silicone liner, or reline the first baking sheet after carefully removing the original liner and brittle.

Melt the chocolate. Using a kitchen fork, toss the brittle, several pieces at a time, into the melted chocolate, making sure each piece is completely coated. Use a wooden spoon to transfer the coated brittle to the plate with the chopped almonds. Coat both sides of the brittle with chopped nuts, then set on the freshly lined baking sheet. Allow chocolate to set.

Store the brittle in an airtight container at room temperature for up to 2 weeks. Yield: 2 lbs.

Creamy, Rich Chocolate-Marshmallow Fudge

There is such a mystique to fudge making that it is always welcome as a homemade gift.

4 tbsp. unsalted butter, melted
1 cup light brown sugar, firmly packed
1 cup granulated sugar
¼ cup light corn syrup
½ cup half-and-half
⅛ tsp. salt
4 oz. semisweet or bittersweet chocolate, coarsely chopped
½ cup walnuts, chopped and lightly toasted
1½ cups mini marshmallows

Bev's Bites

Want the marshmallows on the top? Simply flip over the fudge pieces when serving!

Lightly butter an 8" square pan and set aside.

In a large saucepan over medium heat, combine the butter, brown sugar, granulated sugar, corn syrup, half-and-half, and salt and bring to a boil, stirring constantly. Using a pastry brush dipped in water, brush down any sugar crystals that form on the sides of the pan.

Boil for 2½ minutes, then stir in the chocolate until melted and well blended. Continue to boil, without stirring, until a candy thermometer reads 234 degrees, about 10 minutes.

Remove saucepan from heat and let cool until almost room temperature or 100 degrees on a candy thermometer, about 15 minutes. Using a handheld electric mixer, beat the fudge until the color dulls and the fudge is creamy. Stir in walnuts by hand.

Sprinkle the marshmallows over the bottom of the prepared pan and scrape the fudge over them. Lay a piece of plastic wrap across the surface and, using your hands, press the fudge down into the marshmallows. Remove the plastic wrap and smooth the surface of the fudge with a spatula.

Cover the pan with foil and refrigerate until firm, about 6 hours. Cut into 2" bars (or any shape desired) to serve or give as a gift. Yield: about 16 pieces.

Rocky road ahead? Take some of this fudge along for the ride.

Chocolate Sauce: It Makes Every Day Special!

Everyone loves a chocolate sauce, especially as a homemade gift. All of these sauces can be used for your own delight or poured into jars to give away. Pick and give your faves!

SIMPLY DECADENT WHITE CHOCOLATE SAUCE

2 cups white chocolate, coarsely chopped
¾ cup heavy whipping cream
1 tbsp. plus 1 tsp. light corn syrup

CHOCOLATE ORANGE SAUCE

12 oz. bittersweet chocolate, coarsely shopped
1½ tbsp. orange zest, freshly grated
¼ cup fresh orange juice
½ cup heavy whipping cream
2 tbsp. unsalted butter

DOUBLE CHOCOLATE ESPRESSO SAUCE

9 oz. bittersweet chocolate, coarsely chopped
¾ cup water
¼ cup plus 2 tbsp. granulated sugar
¼ cup light corn syrup
¼ cup unsweetened cocoa powder, sifted
1½ tsp. to 1 tbsp. espresso powder, mixed with 1 tsp. of water

For the Simply Decadent White Chocolate Sauce: Combine the chocolate and cream in the top of a double boiler or in a heatproof bowl on top of a saucepan of hot, not boiling, water. Whisk until the chocolate is melted and the mixture is smooth.

Remove the bowl from the heat and stir in corn syrup. Set the sauce aside to cool. Serve warm or at room temperature. Yield: 3 cups.

For the Chocolate Orange Sauce: Combine the chocolate, orange zest, orange juice, cream, and butter in the top of a double boiler or in a heatproof bowl on top of a saucepan of hot, not boiling, water. Whisk until the chocolate is melted.

Remove the bowl from the heat and whisk until smooth. Use immediately or keep warm until ready to serve. Yield: 2 cups.

For the Double Chocolate Espresso Sauce: Melt the chocolate in the top of a double boiler or in a heatproof bowl on top of a saucepan of hot, not boiling, water. Whisk until smooth.

In a medium saucepan, combine the water with the sugar and corn syrup and bring to a boil over high heat. Whisk in the cocoa powder. Reduce the heat to medium and cook, stirring constantly, until slightly thickened.

Remove the saucepan from the heat and whisk in the melted chocolate and dissolved espresso.

Serve warm or refrigerate for up to 1 week. Yield: 1½ cups.

Chocolate sauce, meet your espresso sidekick!

HOT FUDGE NIBBY SAUCE

1 cup confectioners' sugar, sifted
½ cup unsalted butter, cut into pieces
½ cup heavy whipping cream
4 oz. semisweet chocolate with cocoa nibs, coarsely chopped
4 oz. unsweetened chocolate, coarsely chopped
2 tsp. vanilla extract

DEEP, DARK, DOUBLE CHOCOLATE HOT FUDGE SAUCE

¼ cup unsweetened cocoa powder, sifted
⅔ cup heavy whipping cream
2 cups light corn syrup
1 lb. semisweet chocolate, coarsely chopped
5 tbsp. unsalted butter, cut into pieces
Pinch of salt

Bev's Bites

Always splurge on really good chocolate for these sauces, as the flavor will shine through.

For the Hot Fudge Nibby Sauce: In a medium saucepan, combine the confectioners' sugar, butter, and cream and stir over medium-low heat until smooth.

Remove from heat and add the semisweet and unsweetened chocolates, stirring until melted and smooth. Stir in the vanilla.

Cover and chill. When ready to serve, rewarm over low heat. This may be prepared up to 1 week in advance. Yield: 2 cups.

For the Deep, Dark, Double Chocolate Hot Fudge: In a medium saucepan, whisk together the cocoa powder and heavy cream until smooth. Add the corn syrup, chocolate, butter, and salt. Set the pan over medium heat, stirring occasionally to combine.

When the chocolate is melted and the mixture comes to a boil, reduce heat and let simmer gently until slightly thickened, about 8 minutes.

Let cool until barely warm before pouring into jars or stirring in one of the flavor variations. Yield: 5 cups.

Flavor Variation: Mint
Stir 1½ tsp. pure peppermint extract into the warm sauce.

Flavor Variation: Cinnamon
Whisk ½ tbsp. ground cinnamon into the warm sauce, taste, and add more cinnamon if desired.

Just a hint of cocoa nibs gives this rich sauce a slightly nutty texture—the perfect topping for a hot fudge banana sundae.

Chocolate Coconut Candy Bars
Miniature candy bars, made by you!

¾ cup sweetened flaked coconut
¾ cup unsweetened dried coconut
⅓ cup sweetened condensed milk
4 oz. bittersweet chocolate, melted

Line bottom and sides of an 8" square cake pan with a sheet of waxed paper, leaving a 2-inch overhang.

In a large bowl, mix together the sweetened coconut, unsweetened coconut, and condensed milk until well combined, then firmly press into pan in an even layer. Chill, uncovered, for 5 minutes.

Spread chocolate evenly over the coconut layer with offset spatula and chill until firm, about 10 minutes.

Lift onto a cutting board using the wax paper overhang. Halve bars with a sharp knife. Sandwich halves together, coconut sides in, discarding waxed paper. Cut into 1" squares. Chill, covered, until ready to serve. Yield: 32 pieces.

How to Make a Truffle Sampler

Once you learn how to make truffles, the flavor possibilities are endless. An assortment of three to six varieties wrapped in a cute box makes a fantastic gift—just remember to save some for yourself!

Use simple but elegant Chocolate Truffles with any combination of flavor variations, and you will be sure to make a big hit.

Chocolate Truffles with Flavor Variations

Truffles are perfect as-is in their chocolate splendor, but why not create an extra batch with flavor variations too?

- 20 oz. semisweet chocolate, coarsely chopped, divided
- 1 cup heavy whipping cream
- 2 tbsp. unsalted butter, room temperature
- 1 cup unsweetened Dutch process cocoa powder, sifted, plus additional as needed
- 1 cup toasted nuts (almonds, walnuts, or pecans), finely chopped, if desired

Bev's Bites

In this recipe, truffles are rolled in cocoa powder or ground nuts right after they've been coated with melted chocolate. Dutch process cocoa powder is best for coating the truffles because it is brighter in color and less acidic than natural cocoa powder.

I've found that refrigerating the ganache overnight works best, because once you start rolling the truffles, two hours doesn't seem to keep the chocolate cold enough.

Truffles will keep for up to 5 days in an airtight container in the refrigerator. Bring to room temperature before serving.

Process 12 oz. of the chocolate in a food processor until it reaches the consistency of coarse meal, about 30 seconds.

In a small saucepan, bring the cream to a boil over medium heat. Add the cream to the food processor and process until smooth, about 10 seconds.

Add the butter to the warm (but not hot) chocolate mixture in the food processor. Process until smooth, about 10 seconds. Transfer ganache mixture to a medium bowl. If making a flavor variation, add it here. Cover tightly with plastic wrap and refrigerate until firm, at least 2 hours or overnight.

Line a baking sheet with parchment paper.

Put the cocoa powder in a large bowl. Using a 2 tsp. measure or a small scoop, shape rounded, heaping teaspoonfuls of ganache mixture and drop them onto the prepared baking sheet.

Once all the truffles are scooped, dip them in the cocoa and use your palms to roll the truffles into smooth 1" balls (don't worry about making them perfect, as slightly irregular truffles have an appealing, homemade appearance). Transfer the truffles to the refrigerator for at least 1 hour or until they have re-firmed and are not overly soft.

Melt the remaining 8 oz. of chocolate. Working in batches, use your clean fingers or a few forks to coat the truffles with the melted chocolate.

Coat the truffles again with the remaining cocoa or chopped nuts (if desired) and return them to the baking sheet. If using your hands, you'll have to stop and wash off the chocolate between batches.

Let the truffles sit at room temperature for at least 10 minutes before serving. Yield: 3½ dozen.

Flavor Variation: Candied Orange
1 oz. candied orange peel, finely chopped

Flavor Variation: Ginger
1 oz. candied ginger, finely chopped

Flavor Variation: Jasmine
2 tsp. loose Jasmine tea leaves, finely chopped

Flavor Variation: Liqueur Filling
3 tbsp. flavored liqueur. Need inspiration? Try a fruit-, nut-, coffee-, or chocolate-based liqueur.

Flavor Variation: PB and J
Add ½ to ⅔ cup strawberry jam to the ganache and process until smooth. Coat the truffles with 2 cups ground, salted peanuts.

Flavor Variation: Toffee and Fleur de Sel
Add ½ cup ground toffee bits and ¼ tsp. fleur de sel to the ganache. Coat with 1¼ cups ground toffee bits mixed with 1 tsp. fleur de sel.

The Kid in All Adults Marshmallow Truffles

What fun to give—and serve.

- 7 oz. jar marshmallow crème
- ⅓ cup unsalted butter, room temperature
- 1 tbsp. raspberry or orange liqueur
- ¼ tsp. salt
- 3¼ cups confectioners' sugar, sifted, divided
- About ½ cup toasted almonds, pecan halves, macadamia nuts, hazelnuts (all nuts cut into large pieces), quartered and pitted dates, and/or dried cherries
- 12 oz. semisweet chocolate, coarsely chopped
- 1 tbsp. shortening
- Toasted nuts, finely chopped; toasted coconut; candy sprinkles; or nonpareils, for topping
- 3 oz. white chocolate, melted and warm, for topping

Bev's Bites

To store or give, layer truffles between pieces of wax paper in an airtight container. Store in the refrigerator for up to 1 week or freeze for up to 3 months.

Line a baking sheet with waxed paper and butter the paper. Set aside.

In the large bowl of an electric mixer, combine the marshmallow crème, butter, liqueur, and salt and beat on medium-low speed until smooth. Gradually add 3 cups of the confectioners' sugar, beating until well mixed. Cover and chill about 1 hour or until mixture stays together and is easy to handle.

Lightly dust your hands with the remaining ¼ cup confectioners' sugar and shape marshmallow mixture into 1" balls, forming the mixture around toasted almonds, pecans, or other nuts or dried fruit. Place the balls on the prepared baking sheets. Cover lightly; freeze for 20 minutes.

In a small saucepan, combine the semisweet chocolate and shortening and stir over very low heat until melted and smooth. Remove saucepan from heat.

Line another baking sheet with wax paper. Set aside.

Remove the balls, a few at a time, from the freezer. Dip the balls into chocolate mixture, using a fork to coat them evenly. Draw the fork across the rim of the saucepan to remove excess chocolate.

Place dipped truffles on wax paper-lined baking sheet. Immediately sprinkle tops with finely chopped nuts, toasted coconut, sprinkles, or nonpareils. Let stand at room temperature about 15 minutes or until completely set. Drizzle truffles with melted white chocolate. Yield: 3 dozen.

Fleur de Sel Dark Chocolate Caramel Truffles

As delicious as they are beautiful . . .

20 oz. bittersweet chocolate, finely chopped, divided
⅓ cup granulated sugar
2 tbsp. water
⅔ cup heavy whipping cream
¼ tsp. fleur de sel, plus additional for sprinkling
½ cup unsweetened cocoa powder, sifted

Bev's Bites
These may be made one week ahead, covered, and chilled. Bring to room temperature before serving.

Melt 12 oz. of the chocolate.

In a small saucepan, combine the sugar and water and stir over medium heat until sugar dissolves, occasionally brushing the sides of the pan with a wet pastry brush. Increase heat and boil until syrup is a deep amber color, brushing down sides and swirling pan occasionally.

Carefully add cream (mixture will bubble). Stir over low heat until caramel is smooth. Mix caramel and fleur de sel into melted chocolate. Chill until firm, at least 2 hours or overnight.

Place cocoa powder in a wide bowl. Roll caramel mixture into balls, 1 tbsp. at a time, then roll in cocoa powder to coat. Arrange on lined baking sheet. Cover and chill overnight.

Line a jellyroll pan with foil.

Melt remaining 8 oz. chocolate; allow to cool. Working very quickly, dip one truffle at a time in the melted chocolate. Using a fork, lift out truffle and tap fork against the side of the bowl to allow excess coating to drip off. Transfer truffle to jellyroll pan. Repeat with remaining truffles.

Sprinkle truffles lightly with additional fleur de sel. Let stand at room temperature until coating sets, at least 1 hour. Yield: 2 dozen.

Salt, caramel, chocolate, repeat. Salt, caramel, chocolate, repeat.

Chocolate Gifts

Pop in mouth, close eyes, and let sweet enjoyment begin.

Heavenly Homemade Chocolate Marshmallows

Truly, most people can't believe you can make marshmallows in your own kitchen.

Sweetened cocoa powder, for dusting
1¼ cups water, cold, divided
¼ cup unsweetened cocoa powder, sifted
2 cups granulated sugar
½ cup light corn syrup
3 tbsp. unflavored gelatin
2 large egg whites
1 tsp. vanilla extract
1 tsp. chocolate extract
¼ tsp. salt
Sweetened ground chocolate, for sprinkling

Lightly spray a 9" square cake pan. Lightly dust with sweetened cocoa powder. Set aside.

In a small bowl, boil ¼ cup of the water and combine with unsweetened cocoa powder. Set aside.

In a small saucepan, combine sugar, corn syrup and ½ cup water over medium-high heat, stirring constantly, until sugar is dissolved. Cook without stirring until a candy thermometer reaches 240 degrees.

In a small bowl, combine gelatin and the remaining ½ cup of cold water. Set aside.

In the large bowl of an electric mixer with the whisk attachment, beat the egg whites, vanilla, chocolate extract, and salt on high until stiff peaks form.

In a separate bowl of an electric mixer, combine the gelatin mixture, cocoa powder mixture, and hot sugar syrup mixture. Beat on high speed until mixture is thick and tripled in volume. Fold in the egg white mixture ⅓ at a time. Spread mixture evenly into prepared pan. Sprinkle top with sweetened ground chocolate.

Refrigerate until set, at least 2 hours. Cut into 1½" or 2" squares. Yield: between 16 and 36 pieces.

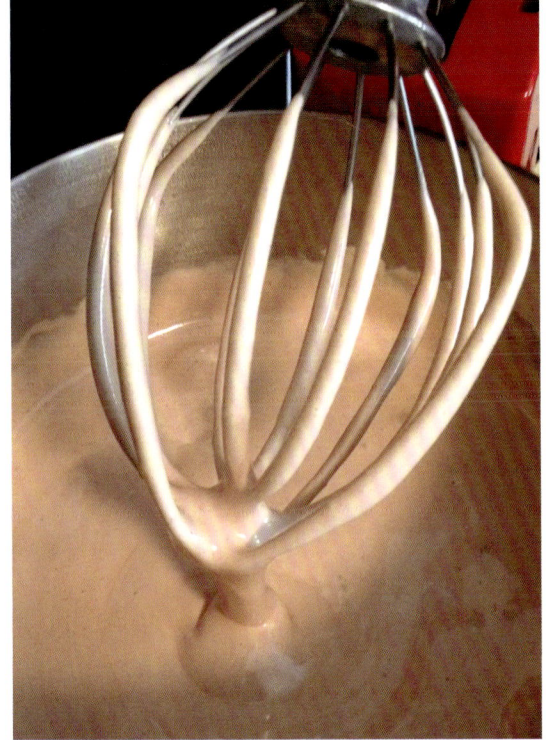

Thick and tripled in volume—marshmallows, we're almost there.

Chocolate Gifts

Bev's Three-Chocolate Bark with Spiced Pecans and Dried Tart Cherries

Some of my friends refer to this as "bark," some as "OMG! I hope you're going to make that again soon," some as "candy." Whatever its name, it is an addictive chocolate extravaganza. Be sure to save some for yourself!

FOR THE PECANS

¼ tsp. sea salt
¼ tsp. cayenne pepper
⅛ tsp. nutmeg, freshly grated
¼ tsp. ground cinnamon
6 tbsp. unsalted butter
¾ cup light brown sugar, firmly packed
2 cups pecan pieces

FOR THE BARK

1 lb. bittersweet chocolate, coarsely chopped
3 tbsp. unsalted butter, divided
1 lb. milk chocolate, coarsely chopped
1 lb. white chocolate, coarsely chopped
2 cups dried tart cherries, snipped into pieces

Bev's Bites

The easiest way to snip the dried cherries into pieces is to use a sharp pair of kitchen scissors.

Store leftovers (??!!) between layers of waxed paper, refrigerated, in an airtight container. This does freeze well and is delicious directly from the freezer (just sayin').

For the Pecans: Heat oven to 400 degrees. Line 2 15" x 10" baking sheets with parchment paper.

In a small bowl, mix together the salt, cayenne, nutmeg, and cinnamon.

In a medium sauté pan, melt butter over medium heat. Add the brown sugar and stir until the sugar dissolves and the mixture is lightly bubbly. Add the pecans and the spice mixture and cook, stirring constantly, until the sugar starts to soften and coat the pecans.

Remove the pan from the heat and spread the mixture over one of the lined baking sheets. Place the pan in the oven and roast for 6 minutes. Remove from the oven and, using a fork, separate the pecan pieces on the parchment paper. Cool completely. Yield: about 2½ cups.

For the Bark: Carefully melt the bittersweet chocolate in the top of a double boiler over gently simmering water, stirring until completely melted. Remove from heat, wipe the bottom of the pot that contains the chocolate, and stir in 1 tbsp. of the butter until completely melted.

Pour the chocolate onto the second prepared baking sheet and spread evenly with an angled metal spatula. Refrigerate, uncovered, for 10 minutes.

While mixture is chilling, melt the milk chocolate in the top of a double boiler over gently simmering water, stirring until completely melted. Remove from heat, wipe the bottom of the pot that contains the chocolate, and stir in 1 tbsp. of the remaining butter until completely melted.

Pour the milk chocolate on top of the bittersweet layer, spreading the chocolate gently, quickly, and evenly with an angled metal spatula. Refrigerate, uncovered, for 10 minutes.

While layers are chilling, melt the white chocolate in the top of a double boiler over gently simmering water, stirring until completely melted. Remove from the heat, wipe the bottom of the pot that contains the chocolate, and stir in the remaining 1 tbsp. of butter until completely melted.

Pour the white chocolate on top of the milk-chocolate layer, spreading the chocolate gently, quickly, and evenly with an angled metal spatula. Sprinkle with the spiced pecans and dried cherry pieces and press them gently but firmly into the white chocolate layer. Place the baking sheet in the refrigerator and chill until the bark sets, at least 3 hours.

When ready to serve, remove bark from the pan and break into pieces using either a chocolate chipper or a sharp knife. Yield: 4 lbs.

Stackable Chocolate-Cookie Hearts

These hearts are crispy and rich with lots of soft, creamy filling.

COOKIES

1¾ cups unbleached, all-purpose flour
⅓ cup unsweetened cocoa powder, sifted
1½ tsp. baking powder
⅔ cup unsalted butter, room temperature, cut into pieces
¾ cup granulated sugar
1 tsp. vanilla
1 large egg
½ cup sour cream

CHOCOLATE-COOKIE BUTTERCREAM

⅔ cup granulated sugar
¼ cup water
4 lightly beaten large egg yolks
1 tsp. vanilla
1 cup unsalted butter, room temperature, cut into pieces
3 oz. bittersweet or semisweet chocolate, melted and cooled

For the Cookies: In a small mixing bowl, stir together the flour, cocoa powder, and baking powder. Set aside.

In the large bowl of an electric mixer, beat the butter on medium-high speed for about 30 seconds. Stop and scrape down the sides of the bowl and beater.

Add the sugar and vanilla and beat until combined. Add the egg, beating until combined.

Alternate adding the flour mixture with the sour cream, beating on low to medium speed after each addition just until combined.

Divide dough in half. Cover and chill in the refrigerator 3 hours or until easy to handle.

Heat oven to 350 degrees. Line a cookie sheet with either parchment paper or a silicone liner.

On a lightly floured surface, roll each half of the dough to about ¼" thickness. Using a 3" heart cookie cutter, cut dough into hearts and place 1" apart on the prepared cookie sheet.

Bake for 6 to 8 minutes or until edges are firm. Cool cookies on cookie sheet for 1 minute, then remove cookies and cool on a wire rack.

For the Buttercream: In a medium saucepan, combine the sugar and water and bring to a boil. Remove from heat.

Place egg yolks in a small bowl. Gradually stir about ½ of the sugar mixture into the egg yolks. Add egg yolk mixture to saucepan.

Bring mixture to a boil, then reduce heat and cook, stirring, for 2 minutes. Remove from heat, then stir in vanilla. Cool to room temperature.

In the large bowl of an electric mixer, beat butter and melted chocolate until light and fluffy. Add cooled sugar mixture, beating until combined. If necessary, chill until spreading consistency is reached.

To assemble cookie sandwiches, spoon and spread buttercream on the bottoms of half of the hearts. Top with the remaining unfrosted cookies, bottom sides down. If desired, pipe some remaining chocolate buttercream around the top edge of each cookie. Refrigerate to store. Yield: 12 to 15 servings.

Puffed and ready to be filled and stacked.

A stackable package of chocolate love!

Chocolate Walnut Fudge

This recipe's tester, Lisa, said that it really gave her biceps a workout. Who knew we should add some chocolate into our workout routine?

- Butter, melted and cooled, for brushing in pan
- 16 oz. semisweet chocolate, finely chopped
- 2 oz. unsweetened chocolate, finely chopped
- ½ tsp. baking soda
- ⅛ tsp. salt
- 14 oz. sweetened condensed milk
- 1 tbsp. vanilla extract
- 1 cup walnuts, coarsely chopped and lightly toasted, plus additional for topping

Bev's Bites

Make sure to remove the bowl from the double boiler before the chocolate is fully melted. If the chocolate stays too long, the chocolate can separate, which would produce greasy fudge.

Line an 8" square baking pan with foil, allowing extra foil to hang over the edge of the pan. Lightly brush foil with butter.

Combine the semisweet and unsweetened chocolate, baking soda, and salt in the top of a large double boiler or a medium heatproof bowl until well mixed. Stir in the condensed milk and vanilla.

Set over a saucepan of hot—not boiling—water and stir with a rubber spatula until the chocolate is almost fully melted but a few small lumps remain.

Remove bowl from heat and continue to stir until the chocolate is fully melted and the mixture is smooth. Stir in the walnuts.

Pour the fudge into the prepared pan and spread in an even layer. Sprinkle with additional walnuts, if desired. Refrigerate until set, about 2 hours. Lift the fudge from the baking pan by using the extra foil as handles. Remove foil. Using a chef's knife, cut into squares. Yield: 16 2" x 2" pieces.

Seriously? One piece of Chocolate Walnut Fudge is all I get?

CHOCOLATE DESSERTS TO DIE FOR!

ELEGANT CHOCOLATE DESSERTS

Elegant and sweet—a small slice of this Sumptuous White Chocolate and Brie Cheesecake goes a long way toward satisfying.

A romantic dinner for two? Entertaining extra-special guests? Elevate your chocolate creations and wow yourself and your guests with these elegant flavors and presentations.

Sumptuous White Chocolate and Brie Cheesecake

Rich and sweet . . . don't we all aspire to be that way?

- 1½ lbs. cream cheese, room temperature, cut into pieces
- 12 oz. Brie cheese or other triple-crème cheese, such as Saint André, room temperature, weighed after rind removed
- ¾ cup granulated sugar
- 5 large eggs, room temperature
- 4 oz. white chocolate, melted and slightly cooled

Bev's Bites

Whip it, whip it good does not apply to cheesecake batter. It is important to avoid over-whipping the filling so that you don't end up with a puffed, cracked cake.

Heat oven to 300 degrees. Lightly grease a 9" springform pan. Line bottom with a lightly greased circle of parchment paper, cut to fit.

In the large bowl of an electric mixer, beat the cream cheese at medium-high speed until smooth. Scrape down the sides of the bowl. Transfer the cheese from the mixing bowl to another bowl and set aside.

In the first mixing bowl, beat the Brie on medium-high speed until completely smooth, stopping often to scrape down the sides of the bowl. With the machine on medium speed, add the cream cheese to the softened Brie, one third at a time. Blend the cheese together until smooth. Reduce speed to low and slowly add the granulated sugar.

At low speed, add the eggs, one at a time. Scrape down the sides of the bowl. On low speed, pour white chocolate into the middle of the bowl and mix until well blended, smooth and creamy. Scrape down the sides of the bowl.

Pour mixture into prepared pan. Place on a heavy rimmed baking pan and pour about ½" of simmering water into the baking pan to form a water bath.

Bake for 1 hour and 15 minutes or until the top is lightly golden brown and puffed. The center should no longer jiggle when the pan is moved. Remove from oven and let cool in the pan for 2 to 4 hours.

To remove cake from the pan, run a thin blade around the edges to loosen. Remove sides of springform pan. Place a piece of parchment or wax paper over the top of the cake and invert onto a plate. Peel the parchment round from the bottom and re-invert the cake onto its serving plate. Remove the top piece of paper.

Serve with seasonal berries or a fresh raspberry coulis. May be stored in the refrigerator for up to one week, as long as no one eats it all. Yield: 10 to 12 servings.

Chocolate Mousse-Filled Meringue Pie

Rich chocolate mousse is captured in a baked meringue crust flavored with a burst of cinnamon.

CRUST

4 large egg whites
½ tsp. cream of tartar
¼ tsp. ground cinnamon
1 cup granulated sugar

FILLING

4 large egg yolks
6 oz. semisweet chocolate, melted
2 tbsp. coffee-flavored liqueur
1 cup heavy whipping cream
¼ cup granulated sugar

White chocolate curls, for garnish

Bev's Bites

To determine if sugar has dissolved for the meringue crust, rub a small amount of meringue between thumb and forefinger. It should be smooth, not grainy.

Create drama—curl your chocolate! Chocolate curls add whimsy to your favorite desserts, whether they're fancy or simple.

For the Crust: Heat oven to 275 degrees. Generously butter a 9" pie pan.

In the large bowl of an electric mixer, beat egg whites, cream of tartar, and cinnamon until frothy.

Add sugar, 2 tbsp. at a time, beating continuously until sugar is dissolved and stiff glossy peaks form, about 8 to 10 minutes. Do not under beat.

Spread evenly over bottom and up sides of prepared pan. Bake for 1 hour, then turn oven off, letting meringue cool in oven for an additional 2 hours. Do not open the oven door!

For the Filling: In a medium bowl, whisk reserved egg yolks into chocolate, one at a time, until well blended. Add liqueur.

In the large bowl of an electric mixer, beat whipping cream until soft peaks form. Add sugar and beat until stiff peaks form. Fold in cooled chocolate mixture.

Spoon filling into cooled meringue shell and refrigerate until set. Cover with plastic wrap and refrigerate an additional 8 hours or overnight before serving.

When ready to serve, decorate with white chocolate curls. Yield: 8 servings.

Chocolate Mousse-Filled Chocolate Cream Puffs

At very special occasions, these cream puffs will be the cream of the crop.

CHOCOLATE MOUSSE

4 large egg yolks
¼ cup granulated sugar
2½ cups heavy whipping cream, divided
6 oz. semisweet chocolate, coarsely chopped

PÂTE À CHOUX SHELLS

¾ cup plus 2 tbsp. unbleached, all-purpose flour
2 tbsp. unsweetened cocoa powder
1 tbsp. granulated sugar
1 cup water
½ cup unsalted butter, cut into pieces
4 large eggs

For the Mousse: Beat egg yolks in the small bowl of an electric mixer on high speed until thick and lemon colored. Gradually beat in sugar.

In a 2-quart saucepan, heat 1 cup of the cream over medium-high heat just until hot. Gradually stir half of the hot cream into the egg yolk mixture, then add egg and cream mixture back into the hot cream in the saucepan.

Cook over low heat for about 5 minutes, stirring constantly until mixture thickens and being careful not to bring to a boil. Stir in chocolate until melted. Cover and refrigerate for about 2 hours, stirring occasionally, just until chilled.

Beat remaining 1½ cups heavy cream in a chilled bowl on high speed until stiff. Fold chocolate mixture into whipped cream. Refrigerate, uncovered, until ready to use. Yield: about 3 cups.

For the Shells: Heat oven to 400 degrees.

Combine flour, cocoa powder, and granulated sugar in a small bowl. Set aside.

In a 2½-quart saucepan, heat the water and butter to a rolling boil. Stir in the flour mixture and reduce heat to low. Stir vigorously over low heat until mixture forms a ball. Remove saucepan from heat. Beat in eggs, all at once, with a spoon, and continue beating until smooth.

Drop dough by scant ¼ cupful about 3" apart on an ungreased cookie sheet. Bake 35 to 40 minutes or until puffed and golden.

With a sharp knife, place a small slit midway on the side of each puff. Return to oven for 10 minutes, then remove and cool on a wire rack away from any draft for about 30 minutes.

Cut off the top ⅓ of each puff. Spoon mousse into puffs, replace tops, and serve. Yield: 12 filled cream puffs.

Elegant Chocolate Desserts

Oh, You Bittersweet Truffle Tart

The Whipped Almond Mascarpone takes this tart over the entertaining edge.

CRUST

⅔ cup unbleached, all-purpose flour
½ cup confectioners' sugar, sifted
½ cup blanched almonds, ground
6 tbsp. unsalted butter, room temperature
⅓ cup unsweetened cocoa powder, sifted

FILLING

1¼ cups heavy whipping cream
12 oz. bittersweet or semisweet chocolate, coarsely chopped
¼ cup granulated sugar
¼ cup strawberry jam

WHIPPED ALMOND MASCARPONE

8 oz. mascarpone cheese
⅔ cup granulated sugar
⅓ cup heavy whipping cream
⅛ tsp. almond extract

For the Crust: Heat oven to 350 degrees.

In the large bowl of an electric mixer, beat the flour, confectioners' sugar, almonds, butter, and cocoa powder until combined. Knead gently with clean hands until mixture comes together.

Press dough onto bottom and up sides of an ungreased, 9" fluted tart pan with removable bottom.

Bake for 12 to 14 minutes or until crust is slightly puffed. Cool in pan on a wire rack.

For the Filling: In a medium saucepan, combine cream, chocolate, and sugar. Cook over medium heat until chocolate is melted, stirring occasionally. Transfer to a medium bowl and whisk in strawberry jam. Cover and chill about 1 hour or until mixture is cooled and slightly thickened, stirring occasionally.

Beat cooled chocolate mixture about 30 seconds or until the color lightens slightly. Pour into crust, spreading evenly. Cover and chill about 2 hours or until firm. Yield: 10 servings.

For the Whipped Almond Mascarpone: In the large bowl of an electric mixer, beat the mascarpone, sugar, heavy cream, and almond extract on medium speed until smooth. Scrape down the sides of the bowl. Beat on high speed until mixture is thick and holds firm peaks. Yield: about 2 cups.

Serve slices of tart topped with whipped almond mascarpone.

Yes, eating a slice of this tart might be bittersweet, but you'll also feel that way once it's gone!

Chocolate Orange Pots de Crème

A creamy, intense chocolate pudding with a burst of orange flavor is a scrumptious way to end a meal.

⅔ cup milk, whole
½ cup heavy whipping cream
1 tbsp. Grand Marnier or other orange liqueur
1 tsp. vanilla extract
1 tsp. orange zest, finely grated
4 oz. bittersweet or semisweet chocolate, coarsely chopped
4 large egg yolks
3 tbsp. granulated sugar

Bev's Bites
These may be made 2 days ahead if kept refrigerated.

Heat oven to 350 degrees.

In a medium saucepan, bring the milk, heavy cream, Grand Marnier, vanilla, and orange zest to a boil. Remove saucepan from heat. Add chocolate and stir until melted and smooth.

Whisk egg yolks and sugar in a medium bowl until the mixture turns pale yellow. Whisk egg mixture into chocolate mixture, then strain into a 2-cup measuring cup.

Divide mixture between 2 8-oz. custard cups. Place cups in a small baking dish and add enough water to the baking dish to come halfway up the sides of the cups. Cover baking dish tightly with foil.

Bake until custard is set, about 40 minutes. Remove cups from water in dish and place in refrigerator, uncovered, until cool. Cover with plastic wrap and refrigerate until cold, about 6 hours. Yield: 2 servings.

Swirls-of-Chocolate Meringues

I love every bit of these: the look, the crunchy outside, the soft inside . . .

4 large egg whites, room temperature
1 cup granulated sugar
3 oz. bittersweet chocolate, melted and slightly cooled

Heat oven to 275 degrees. Line two baking sheets with parchment paper.

Combine egg whites and sugar in a bowl and place over a saucepan with barely simmering water. Whisk until mixture is hot, about 5 to 8 minutes.

Transfer egg mixture to the large bowl of an electric mixer, warmed, and beat on high speed until stiff peaks form and mixture is lukewarm, 5 to 8 minutes.

Remove bowl from mixer and drizzle melted chocolate over the egg whites, folding in with a rubber spatula just until mixture is marbled.

Drop batter in large mounds by the tablespoonful spaced 2" apart on the prepared baking sheets.

Bake until the outside is crunchy and the inside is still chewy, about 35 minutes. Transfer pans to a wire rack to cool completely before removing meringues from parchment paper. Store in an airtight container. Yield: 24 to 26 meringues.

One bite of these crunchy-on-the-outside and soft-on-the-inside chocolaty meringues and you'll fall in love all over again.

Elegant Chocolate Desserts

Triple-Decker Chocolate Cookies

Three times the fun and three times the chocolate—that is my kind of cookie!

COOKIE

- ½ cup unsalted butter, room temperature, cut into pieces
- ¾ cup granulated sugar
- ¼ cup dark brown sugar, firmly packed
- ½ tsp. baking soda
- ⅛ tsp. salt
- ⅛ tsp. ground black pepper
- 1 large egg
- 2 tsp. vanilla extract
- 1⅓ cups unbleached, all-purpose flour
- ½ cup unsweetened cocoa powder, sifted

GANACHE

- ⅓ cup plus 2 tbsp. heavy whipping cream
- 6 ounces bittersweet chocolate, coarsely chopped

Bev's Bites

Store cookie stacks in an airtight container in the refrigerator for up to 2 days.

For the Cookie: In the large bowl of an electric mixer, beat the butter to soften. Scrape down the sides of the bowl. Add the granulated sugar, brown sugar, baking soda, salt, and pepper; beat until combined. Scrape down the sides of the bowl, then beat in egg and vanilla.

In a small bowl, whisk together the flour and cocoa powder. Gradually beat flour mixture into the egg mixture. Divide dough into two portions and shape each portion of dough into a 1½"-diameter log (it will end up being about 8" long). Wrap each log in plastic wrap and chill for 1 hour or freeze for 30 minutes (until firm enough to slice).

Heat oven to 350 degrees.

Work with one roll at a time. Unwrap chilled dough and cut into slices about ¼" thick. Place slices 2" apart on ungreased cookie sheets. Bake for 6 to 7 minutes or until edges are set. Cool on cookie sheet for 1 minute, then transfer cookies to a wire rack to cool completely.

For the Ganache: In a small saucepan, bring the heavy cream to a simmer (do not boil).

Place chocolate in a medium bowl. Pour hot cream over chocolate, allow to soften for 10 minutes, and then stir until mixture is melted and smooth. Let stand about 20 minutes or until mixture thickens enough to spread. Yield: about 1 cup.

To build cookies: For each triple-decker stack, spread 1 tsp. ganache evenly over the bottom side of one cookie. Place a plain cookie on top of ganache. Spread top with 1 tsp. ganache and top with another cookie, top side up. Once all cookies are sandwiched, pipe remaining ganache over top of cookies. Chill for 30 minutes to set. Yield: 12 to 14 triple-decker cookies.

It takes a big mouth and a large napkin to properly enjoy these triple-decker chocolate delights.

Melt-in-Your-Mouth Chocolate Almond Wafers

I served these at a dinner party and the men asked for seconds and thirds.

DOUGH

- 1 cup granulated sugar
- ¾ cup unsalted butter, room temperature, cut into pieces
- 3 oz. unsweetened chocolate, melted
- 1 large egg
- 1 tsp. almond extract
- 1¼ cups unbleached, all-purpose flour
- 1 tsp. baking powder
- ½ tsp. salt
- ½ cup blanched almonds, chopped

GLAZES

- 2 oz. bittersweet chocolate, coarsely chopped
- 2 tsp. shortening, divided
- 2 oz. white chocolate, coarsely chopped

For the Dough: In the large bowl of an electric mixer, beat the sugar, butter, chocolate, egg, and almond extract at medium speed until creamy. Scrape down the sides of the bowl.

Reduce speed to low and add flour, baking powder, and salt, beating until well mixed. Scrape down the sides of the bowl. Stir in almonds.

Divide dough in half. On wax paper, shape each half into a 12" x 1¼" roll. Wrap in plastic wrap and refrigerate until firm, at least 2 hours or overnight.

Heat oven to 350 degrees.

Cut rolls into ¼"-thick slices. Place 1" apart on ungreased cookie sheets. Bake for 10 to 12 minutes or until set. Allow to cool completely on a wire rack. Yield: 5½ dozen cookies.

For the Glazes: Melt bittersweet chocolate with 1 tsp. of the shortening, mixing to blend.

Repeat, in a separate bowl, with white chocolate and remaining 1 tsp. of shortening. Yield: about ¼ cup each.

Drizzle cooled cookies with both chocolate glazes. Allow glazes to set before serving.

Four-Ways-with-Chocolate Tiramisu

1-2 3-oz. packages ladyfingers, split if using soft cookies
½ cup brewed espresso, divided
8 oz. mascarpone cheese
1 cup heavy whipping cream
¼ cup confectioners' sugar
1 tsp. vanilla extract
⅓ cup chocolate liqueur
2 oz. white chocolate, grated
2 oz. bittersweet chocolate, grated
Unsweetened cocoa powder, for dusting

Line the bottom of an 8" square cake pan tightly with some of the ladyfingers, cutting to fit as needed.

Drizzle half of the espresso evenly over cookies. Set aside.

In the large bowl of an electric mixer, beat together the mascarpone, heavy cream, confectioners' sugar, and vanilla until stiff peaks form. Beat in the chocolate liqueur just until combined.

Spoon half of the mascarpone mixture over espresso-soaked ladyfingers, spreading evenly. Sprinkle white chocolate and bittersweet chocolate over the mascarpone mixture. Top with another layer of ladyfingers.

Pour the remaining espresso over the cookies. Top with remaining mascarpone mixture. Cover and chill for 8 to 24 hours. When ready to serve, sift a generous amount of cocoa powder over top of dessert. Yield: 9 to 12 servings.

"Four? Really?" he asked, doubting.
"Chocolate liqueur, white chocolate, bittersweet chocolate, and cocoa powder,"
she replied, not willing to share.

Elegant Chocolate Desserts

Baked Chocolate Espresso Shots

The perfect way to get your chocolate and espresso fixes, conveniently in one delicious package.

COOKIE DOUGH

¼ cup unsalted butter, room temperature
¼ cup shortening
2 oz. cream cheese, room temperature
1 cup light brown sugar, firmly packed
½ tsp. baking powder
½ tsp. salt
½ tsp. ground cinnamon
¼ tsp. ground nutmeg
1 large egg
2 tsp. vanilla extract
2½ cups unbleached, all-purpose flour

CHOCOLATE GANACHE

⅓ cup heavy whipping cream
1 tsp. instant espresso powder
3 oz. semisweet chocolate, coarsely chopped

FILLING

5 oz. semisweet chocolate, coarsely chopped
2 tbsp. unsalted butter
⅓ cup light brown sugar, firmly packed
1 tbsp. coffee liqueur
2 tsp. vanilla extract
1 tsp. ground cinnamon
1½ tsp. instant espresso powder
¼ tsp. ground nutmeg
1 large egg

For the Cookie Dough: In the large bowl of an electric mixer, beat the butter, shortening, and cream cheese on medium-high speed until light and fluffy. Add brown sugar, baking powder, salt, cinnamon, and nutmeg. Beat until combined. Scrape down the sides of the bowl. Beat in egg and vanilla. Stir in flour by hand just until combined.

Heat oven to 325 degrees.

Shape dough into 36 1¼" balls. Press evenly onto the bottoms and up sides of ungreased 1¾" muffin cups.

For the Ganache: In a small saucepan, combine the cream and espresso powder; bring to a boil. Remove from heat. Add the chocolate and let stand for 5 minutes without stirring, then stir until smooth. Yield: about 1 cup.

For the Filling: In a small saucepan, combine the chocolate and butter. Cook and stir over low heat until melted. Remove from heat and stir in brown sugar, coffee liqueur, vanilla, cinnamon, espresso powder, nutmeg, and egg. Spoon one slightly rounded teaspoon of filling into each pastry-lined muffin cup.

Bake for 20 to 25 minutes or until filling is puffed and set and pastry is just firm. Cool in muffin cups on wire racks for 5 minutes. Carefully remove tarts from muffin cups and cool completely on wire rack. Spoon ganache over tarts. Yield: 33 tarts.

Saddle up to the dessert bar for some of these baked shots.

Naked Chocolate Macaroons

Some macaroons are filled, some are covered and dipped, but these—these are naked!

- 1 lb. confectioners' sugar, sifted
- 2 cups whole blanched almonds
- 6 tbsp. unsweetened cocoa powder, sifted
- ¾ cup (about 6) large egg whites, room temperature

Bev's Bites

No pastry bag? Place the batter into a quart-size resealable zip-top bag. Snip a small edge off of a corner and proceed to press and "pipe" onto prepared sheets.

Heat oven to 400 degrees. Line two baking sheets with parchment paper.

Blend confectioners' sugar and almonds in a food processor until nuts are ground to a powder, scraping down the sides of the bowl often. Add cocoa powder and blend 1 additional minute.

In the large bowl of an electric mixer with the whisk attachment, beat egg whites until stiff but not dry. Fold nut mixture into egg whites in four additions, making a thick batter.

Spoon half of the batter into a pastry bag fitted with a ½" plain tip. Pipe batter onto prepared sheets in 12 walnut-size mounds, spacing mounds 2" apart, as cookies will spread. Bake, one sheet at a time, until macaroons are firm to the touch in the center and dry and cracked on top, about 11 to 12 minutes. Cool on wire rack before removing. Repeat with remaining batter. Yield: 3 to 4 dozen, depending on size made.

Cracked-Top Chocolate Torta

This easy-to-make torta is best eaten the same day it's made (in case you had any doubts).

1 cup unsweetened cocoa powder, sifted
¾ cup granulated sugar
1 cup water
⅓ cup light olive oil
1 large egg
1 large egg white
1 tsp. vanilla extract
1 cup unbleached, all-purpose flour
¼ cup cornstarch
1¼ tsp. baking soda
¼ tsp. salt
Confectioners' sugar, sifted, for sprinkling
Slices of fresh plums, for serving

Heat oven to 325 degrees. Lightly oil a 9" springform pan.

In a large bowl, combine the cocoa powder and sugar, stirring until blended. Whisk in water until smooth, then whisk in olive oil, egg, egg white, and vanilla.

In a small bowl, combine the flour, cornstarch, baking soda, and salt. Whisk flour mixture into cocoa mixture until smooth. Pour into prepared pan.

Bake 45 to 50 minutes or until a toothpick inserted in the center comes out clean. The top should look cracked. Cool in pan on wire rack.

Loosen cake from sides of pan with a small spatula. Transfer cake to a serving plate and sprinkle generously with confectioners' sugar.

To serve, cut into small wedges with slices of fresh plums. Yield: 10 servings.

This light, olive oil torta is the perfect canvas for the tart and sweet flavors of fresh seasonal plums or any of your favorite in-season fruits.

White Chocolate Coeur à la Crème with Chocolate-Covered Espresso Beans

Coeur à la crème is a French concoction that is both earthy and elegant, rustic and dressy—appropriate for any occasion.

12 oz. mascarpone, softened
1¼ cups heavy whipping cream, divided
2 oz. white chocolate, melted and cooled
1 tsp. vanilla extract
1 tsp. fresh lemon juice
1 tbsp. Chambord or other raspberry liqueur
½ cup confectioners' sugar, sifted
Chocolate-covered espresso beans, for serving

Bev's Bites
One large (16 oz.) perforated heart-shaped ceramic mold lined with cheesecloth will be needed to create this dessert. The perforated mold allows the excess liquid (the whey) to drop through the cheesecloth, leaving the delicious "heart" of the cream.

Cut a piece of cheesecloth larger than a 16 oz. perforated, heart-shaped mold. Dampen and wring out lightly. Press into mold and set aside.

In the large bowl of an electric mixer, whip the mascarpone, ¼ cup of the heavy cream, white chocolate, vanilla, lemon juice, and Chambord until thoroughly blended. Refrigerate.

In a small bowl, whip the remaining 1 cup of heavy cream and the confectioners' sugar until the mixture forms stiff peaks. With a rubber spatula, fold the whipped cream into the chilled cheese mixture in 3 batches. Spoon the finished mixture into the prepared mold and fold the edges of the cheesecloth over the top of the mixture. Lightly tap the bottom of the mold on the counter to remove any air spaces between the mixture and the mold.

Refrigerate on a tray or baking sheet for a minimum of 3 hours and up to two days.

When ready to serve, unfold the cheesecloth and drape it over the sides of the mold. Invert mold onto a serving plate. While pressing down on the corners of the cheesecloth, carefully lift off the mold. Remove the cheesecloth slowly. Garnish each serving with chocolate-covered espresso beans. Yield: 6 to 8 servings.

I give you my heart on a platter. Wait—may I have a little back?

Chocolate Spice Route and Macadamia Tart

A perfect change-of-pace dessert for entertaining.

CRUST

6 tbsp. unsalted butter, cold, cut into pieces
⅓ cup granulated sugar
1¾ cups unbleached, all-purpose flour
Pinch of salt
2 large egg yolks

FILLING

¾ cup unsalted butter, melted and cooled
2 large eggs
1 cup granulated sugar
½ cup unbleached, all-purpose flour
¼ tsp. salt
½ tsp. ground cinnamon
¼ tsp. ground allspice
¼ tsp. ground nutmeg
1 cup semisweet chocolate chips
1½ cups unsalted or salted macadamia nuts

Slices of fresh pineapple, for serving

Heat oven to 400 degrees.

For the Crust: In a food processor, combine the butter, sugar, flour, and salt and pulse for 15 seconds or until the mixture forms pea-size clumps. Add the egg yolks and pulse until a crumbly dough forms.

Transfer to an 11" tart pan with removable bottom. Press the crumbs into the bottom and up the sides of the pan. Freeze the crust for 30 minutes.

For the Filling: In a large bowl, combine the butter, eggs, and sugar and whisk well. Add the flour, salt, cinnamon, allspice, and nutmeg and whisk to combine. Stir in the chocolate chips. Pour filling into the chilled tart crust. Sprinkle the macadamias evenly over the top of the filling.

Bake the tart for 10 minutes, then lower the oven to 350 degrees. Continue baking until the nuts and crust are browned, the filling is firm, and the chocolate has melted, about 25 to 30 minutes.

Transfer the tart to a wire cooling rack and cool completely. Remove tart ring and serve at room temperature with slices of fresh pineapple. Yield: 12 servings.

Open the spice cupboard and pull out the classics for this rich and exotic tart.

Macaroon Tarts with Chocolate Cream

Quick and easy, these bite-size treats are extra special.

CRUST

1½ cups shredded, unsweetened coconut
¼ cup granulated sugar
2 large egg whites

FILLING

¼ cup unsalted butter, room temperature
1⅔ cups confectioners' sugar, sifted
2 tbsp. heavy whipping cream
¼ tsp. almond extract
1 tbsp. light corn syrup
2 oz. unsweetened chocolate, melted and cooled

¼ cup sliced almonds, toasted, for garnish

For the Crust: Heat oven to 350 degrees. Lightly spray 12 mini muffin cups with nonstick cooking spray.

In a large bowl, combine the coconut, granulated sugar, and egg whites and mix well to combine. Press 1 tbsp. coconut mixture into each cup.

Bake for 12 to 15 minutes or until crusts just begin to brown. Cool slightly, about 5 to 10 minutes. Remove from pan and cool completely on a wire rack.

For the Filling: In the large bowl of an electric mixer, beat the butter until creamy. Continue beating, alternating between gradually adding the confectioners' sugar, heavy cream, and almond extract, stopping to scrape down the sides of the bowl often. Blend until mixture is light and fluffy. Add corn syrup and mix well. Stir in melted chocolate.

Place filling in a pastry bag fitted with a star tip. Pipe evenly into coconut crusts and garnish with sliced almonds. Yield: 12 tartlets.

Chocolate Crème Brûlée

Duplicate your favorite restaurant dessert at home.

1¾ cups half-and-half
1¾ cups heavy whipping cream, divided
12 tbsp. granulated sugar, divided
4 oz. bittersweet chocolate, coarsely chopped
8 large egg yolks
Pinch of salt
8 tsp. light brown sugar

Heat oven to 350 degrees.

In a medium saucepan, stir together half-and-half, ¾ cup cream, and 6 tbsp. granulated sugar over high heat until mixture begins to boil. Remove saucepan from heat.

Add chocolate and let stand 5 minutes, then whisk until melted and smooth.

In a medium bowl, whisk together egg yolks, salt, and remaining 6 tbsp. granulated sugar. Gradually whisk hot cream mixture into egg mixture. Whisk in remaining 1 cup cream.

Divide mixture among eight ¾-cup ramekins and place in a large roasting pan. Add enough water to the pan to come halfway-up sides of ramekins. Cover pan loosely with foil.

Bake until custards are set around the edges, about 1 hour 10 minutes. Centers should still move slightly when cups are gently shaken. Remove ramekins from water and transfer to the refrigerator to chill, uncovered, until cold. When cold, cover and chill overnight.

To serve, sprinkle the top of each custard with 1 tsp. brown sugar. Caramelize with a kitchen blowtorch until melted and dark golden brown. Yield: 8 servings.

Chocolate Soup with Fruit Salsa or Toasted Nuts

A cross between hot chocolate and pudding, this dessert soup is a perfect end to an elegant dinner.

SOUP

4 cups milk, whole
14 oz. can sweetened condensed milk
11½ oz. semisweet chocolate, coarsely chopped
¼ cup Kahlua or other coffee-flavored liqueur
½ tsp. salt
2 tsp. vanilla extract
1 tsp. espresso powder

FRUIT SALSA

½ cup fresh strawberries, diced
½ cup fresh pineapple, diced
½ cup kiwi, diced
1 tsp. superfine sugar

Freshly whipped cream, for serving
Pistachios, pecan, or almonds, lightly toasted and salted, for serving

Bev's Bites

Here we serve the soup warm, but feel free to serve it at room temperature or cold for equally delicious results.

For the Soup: Combine the whole milk, condensed milk, chocolate, Kahlua, and salt in a saucepan. Bring to a simmer over medium-low heat, whisking constantly.

Reduce heat to low and cook, whisking often, until chocolate melts and mixture is smooth, about 20 minutes.

In a small bowl, whisk together the vanilla and espresso powder until dissolved.

Remove the soup from heat. Stir in espresso mixture. Yield: 6 servings.

For the Salsa: In a medium bowl, toss together the strawberries, pineapple, kiwi, and sugar. Allow to stand for 10 minutes before using. Yield: about 1½ cups.

To serve, garnish soup with a dollop of salsa or a quenelle of freshly whipped cream and a sprinkling of toasted nuts.

A thin layer of soup with whipped cream quenelles and nuts or fruit salsa puts the wow back in dessert.

Individual Chocolate Soufflés

Your guests will love that you lavish such individual attention on them!

4 oz. bittersweet chocolate, coarsely chopped
½ cup heavy whipping cream
3 large egg yolks
½ tsp. vanilla extract
5 large egg whites, room temperature
¼ cup granulated sugar, plus extra for ramekins
Confectioners' sugar, sifted, for serving

In a medium saucepan, melt the chocolate and heavy cream over low heat, stirring until smooth. Remove the saucepan from heat and whisk in the egg yolks, one at a time, blending well after each addition. Stir in the vanilla.

Heat oven to 425 degrees. Butter 6 ⅔-cup ramekins or custard cups and freeze until butter is solid, firm, and set. Butter ramekins again and sprinkle each with granulated sugar.

Rewarm the chocolate mixture over medium-low heat, stirring, just until hot to the touch.

In the medium bowl of an electric mixer, beat the egg whites until soft peaks form. Add the granulated sugar and continue beating until the eggs are glossy and firm. Stir ¼ of the egg whites into the chocolate mixture, then fold the remaining egg whites into the chocolate mixture just until combined.

Scrape the soufflé mixture into the prepared ramekins, smooth the surfaces, and run your clean thumb around the inside rim of each ramekin. Set the ramekins on a baking sheet and bake the soufflés in the middle of the oven for about 8 minutes until puffed and set around the edges.

Dust with confectioners' sugar and serve at once. Yield: 6 servings.

Chocolate Sauce

Delicious accompaniments to individual chocolate soufflés.

1 cup heavy whipping cream
8 oz. bittersweet chocolate, finely chopped
2 tbsp. unsalted butter

In a small saucepan, bring the cream to a gentle boil.

Place the chocolate in a medium bowl. Pour the hot cream over the chocolate and let the mixture stand for 30 seconds to melt the chocolate. Gently stir until smooth.

Add the butter and continue stirring until incorporated. Yield: 1 cup.

Decadent White Chocolate Pastry Cream

This is a delicious, go-to topping for brownies, cake slices, or individual soufflés.

4 cups heavy whipping cream, divided
½ cup granulated sugar
4 tsp. cornstarch or arrowroot
4 large egg yolks
2 tsp. vanilla extract
8 oz. white chocolate, coarsely chopped

In a small saucepan over medium heat, bring 2 cups of the cream to a simmer. Place remaining 2 cups of cream in the refrigerator to cool. Remove saucepan from heat.

In the large bowl of an electric mixer, beat together the sugar, cornstarch or arrowroot, and egg yolks until light and creamy. Slowly add warm cream, beating continuously.

Scrape contents of bowl back into the saucepan. Add vanilla. Cook over medium heat, stirring constantly. Mixture is ready when it thickens enough to coat the back of a metal spoon.

Remove saucepan from heat and quickly stir in chocolate until melted and blended. Set aside to cool.

When ready to use, beat the remaining 2 cups cold cream at high speed until stiff peaks form. Fold whipped cream into white chocolate mixture. Yield: 4 cups.

White Chocolate Mousse with Strawberry Coulis

Serve this as a dessert unto itself or as an accompaniment to an unembellished cake.

WHITE CHOCOLATE MOUSSE

2 cups heavy whipping cream
6 oz. white chocolate, coarsely chopped
1 tsp. vanilla extract

STRAWBERRY COULIS

¼ cup water
12 oz. fresh or frozen strawberries, thawed, quartered, and hulled
3 tbsp. granulated sugar
2 tsp. fresh lemon juice

For the Mousse: In a medium saucepan, combine the cream and chocolate and cook over low heat, stirring constantly, until smooth. Remove saucepan from heat and stir in vanilla. Transfer mixture to a large bowl. Cool 10 minutes, then cover with plastic wrap and refrigerate, stirring occasionally, for 6 hours or overnight until mixture is very cold and thickened.

In the large bowl of an electric mixer, beat the cream mixture at high speed just until light and fluffy. Do not overbeat or mixture will separate. Serve chilled, topped with strawberry coulis. Yield: 6 servings.

For the Coulis: Combine the water, strawberries, sugar, and lemon juice in a blender and blend until smooth. Cover and refrigerate until cold, at least 2 hours. Yield: 1¾ cups.

Downsized Chocolate Decadence

Consider this dessert as an elegant option for mid-week entertaining.

¼ cup unsalted butter, cut into pieces
¼ cup semisweet chocolate, coarsely chopped
2 tbsp. water
2 large eggs
1 tbsp. granulated sugar
1 tbsp. unsweetened cocoa powder, Dutch process
Strawberry coulis, for serving (see Index)

Heat oven to 350 degrees. Lightly butter a 6" cake pan. Set pan on 2 sheets of foil about 10" square. Lift foil edges and press firmly against pan with edges extending above pan rim; set in a larger baking pan.

In a 1½-quart saucepan over low heat, stir the butter, chocolate, and water until smooth. Remove from heat and let cool.

Add eggs, sugar, and cocoa powder to saucepan and beat until well mixed. Pour batter into cake pan.

Carefully pour ½" boiling water into outer pan. Bake until center of cake feels set when gently touched, about 30 minutes. Using the foil, lift cake onto a wire rack. When cool, remove foil. Cover and chill at least 30 minutes or overnight.

Cut cake into wedges and serve with strawberry coulis. Yield: 3 or 4 servings.

Chocolate Pavlova

I'm always a huge fan of anything with meringue, and this crisp, chocolaty wonder is ballerina-worthy.

MERINGUE

- 3 large eggs whites
- ¾ cup granulated sugar
- 2 tbsp. unsweetened cocoa powder, sifted
- 1 tsp. cornstarch
- ½ tsp. instant coffee granules
- 1 tsp. vinegar
- 1 tsp. water

FILLING

- 6 oz. semisweet chocolate, coarsely chopped
- 2 oz. unsweetened chocolate, coarsely chopped
- ¼ cup granulated sugar
- ¼ cup water
- 3 large egg yolks
- 3 tbsp. amaretto
- 2 cups heavy whipping cream, whipped

For the Meringue: Heat oven to 275 degrees. Line cookie sheets with parchment paper or silicone liners.

In the large bowl of an electric mixer, beat egg whites until foamy. Gradually add sugar, cocoa powder, cornstarch, and coffee, beating until stiff peaks form. Fold in vinegar and water.

To form meringue shells, place heaping tablespoonfuls of egg mixture on prepared cookie sheets, spacing 1" to 2" apart. Spread mixture into a 3½"-diameter circle. Make a deep indentation in each shell.

Bake for 45 minutes or until outside edges are slightly dry. Turn oven off, but leave shells in the oven with the door closed for 2 hours. Remove from oven and cool completely on wire racks.

For the Filling: In a small saucepan over low heat, combine semisweet chocolate, unsweetened chocolate, sugar, and water; stir until chocolate is melted and sugar is dissolved. Cool slightly. Place chocolate mixture in the container of a blender. Add egg yolks and amaretto and blend until smooth, about 1 minute.

Place chocolate mixture in a large bowl, then fold whipped cream into chocolate mixture. Chill.

To serve, spoon chocolate filling into meringue shells. Yield: 12 servings.

Mascarpone Chocolate Fondue

This fondue is simple to make and spectacular to serve.

⅔ cup plus 2 tbsp. milk, whole or 2%
4 tbsp. chocolate liqueur
8 oz. mascarpone cheese
2 cups bittersweet chocolate, coarsely chopped
Pinch of salt
Dippers (cubed pound cake, fresh strawberries, pretzel sticks, raspberries, large blackberries, fresh pineapple chunks, toasted cubes of angel food cake), for serving

Combine the milk, chocolate liqueur, mascarpone, chocolate, and salt in the container of a Vitamix blender. Secure lid. Select Variable 1 and slowly increase speed to Variable 10, then High, using the tamper to press ingredients into the blades. Blend for about 3 minutes or until mixture is hot.

Spoon into fondue pot to keep warm. Serve with dippers. Yield: 6 to 8 servings.

Alternately: In a medium saucepan, combine the milk, chocolate liqueur, mascarpone, chocolate, and salt. Cook over medium-low heat, stirring constantly, until mixture is melted and smooth.

Transfer mixture to fondue pot and keep warm. Serve with dippers. Yield: 6 to 8 servings.

Intense dark chocolate balances the creamy, rich texture of mascarpone cheese in this decadently easy fondue.

Java Jolt Chocolate Sandwich Cookies

Large or small—the size of the jolt depends on how large you make the cookies!

CHOCOALTE ESPRESSO COOKIES

1 cup unbleached, all-purpose flour
¼ cup unsweetened cocoa powder, sifted, not Dutch process
½ tsp. baking soda
⅛ tsp. salt
1¾ tsp. instant espresso powder
1½ tsp. vanilla extract
½ cup unsalted butter, room temperature, cut into pieces
½ cup granulated sugar
½ cup light brown sugar, firmly packed
1 large egg

CHOCOLATE ESPRESSO CREAM FILLING

⅓ cup heavy whipping cream
½ tsp. instant espresso powder
5 oz. bittersweet chocolate, finely chopped

Bev's Bites

Once baked, the cookies can be stored up to 3 days in an airtight container.

For the Cookies: Heat oven to 350 degrees. Line two cookie sheets with parchment paper.

In a medium bowl, whisk together the flour, cocoa powder, baking soda, and salt.

In a small bowl, combine the espresso powder and vanilla and stir until the espresso powder is completely dissolved.

In the large bowl of an electric mixer, beat the butter with the granulated sugar and brown sugar until light and fluffy. Scrape down the sides of the bowl. Beat in the egg until well blended. Beat in the espresso mixture.

With the mixer on low speed, beat in the flour mixture in 3 additions.

Drop dough by the slightly rounded teaspoonful onto the prepared cookie sheets, spacing the cookies about 1½" apart.

Bake for 9 to 13 minutes, switching position of cookie sheets (top to bottom and front to back) halfway through baking, until the edges of the cookies are lightly browned but the centers are still slightly soft. The longer you bake the cookies, the crisper they will be. Let cool on cookie sheets for 2 minutes, then transfer the cookies to a wire rack to cool completely.

For the Filling: In a small saucepan, combine the cream and espresso powder and bring to a boil, stirring to dissolve the espresso powder.

Place chocolate in a food processor. With the food processor running, add the hot cream mixture and process just until the chocolate is completely melted, stopping once or twice to scrape down the sides of the bowl.

Transfer the filling to another bowl and let stand at room temperature, stirring occasionally, until cooled and thickened to a spreadable consistency, about 40 minutes.

To assemble cookies: turn half the cookies upside down and spread a slightly rounded teaspoonful of filling on the bottom of each one, leaving about a ¼" border around the edges.

Top with remaining cookies, right side up, and gently press them together. Let stand for about 30 minutes to set the filling. Yield: 24 sandwich cookies.

Chocolate Espresso Cream Filling? Licking the bowl when no one is looking is definitely optional . . . but I certainly couldn't resist.

Silky and smooth and easy to make . . . forget the box and craft some real chocolate pudding today.

Triple Chocolate Pudding

If you think serving chocolate pudding to guests is too ordinary, think again. This Triple Chocolate Pudding is rich and silky—and yes, they'll love it!

1 cup granulated sugar
6 tbsp. unsweetened Dutch cocoa powder, sifted
⅓ cup unbleached, all-purpose flour
⅛ tsp. salt
2 large egg yolks, lightly beaten
2 cups milk, whole
3 oz. bittersweet or semisweet chocolate, finely chopped
1 oz. milk chocolate, finely chopped
2 tbsp. unsalted butter, room temperature, cut into small pieces
1 tsp. vanilla
Whipped cream, for serving

In a medium saucepan, stir together the sugar, cocoa powder, flour, and salt using a wire whisk.

In a medium bowl, stir together the egg yolks and milk using a wire whisk, then gradually whisk milk mixture into sugar-cocoa mixture until blended.

Place saucepan over medium-low heat and cook, stirring constantly with a heatproof spatula, for 8 to 10 minutes or until custard is thickened and smooth. *Do not allow mixture to boil.*

Remove pan from heat and immediately strain mixture through a sieve into a heatproof medium bowl. Stir in the bittersweet or semisweet chocolate, milk chocolate, butter, and vanilla, mixing until smooth.

Pour pudding into 4 to 6 serving dishes. Lay a sheet of wax paper or plastic wrap directly on the surface of each serving and refrigerate until cold, 2 to 3 hours.

Uncover and top each pudding with a large dollop of whipped cream. Yield: 4 to 6 servings.

Elegant Chocolate Desserts

Deep Dark Chocolate Truffle Cake

This is the perfect slice when only something rich, dense, deep, and dark will do.

- 1 lb. bittersweet chocolate, coarsely chopped
- ½ cup unsalted butter, cut into pieces, room temperature
- 6 large eggs, separated, room temperature
- ½ cup granulated sugar
- ½ cup heavy whipping cream
- 2 tbsp. chocolate liqueur
- 1 tsp. vanilla
- Chunks of fresh pineapple, for serving
- Unsweetened whipped cream, for serving

Heat oven to 350 degrees. Lightly butter a 10" springform pan.

Melt the chocolate and butter; remove from heat and allow to cool for 10 minutes.

In the large bowl of an electric mixer, beat the egg yolks and sugar until thick and yellow-colored. Stop and scrape down the sides of the bowl and beater.

Add cooled chocolate mixture, cream, chocolate liqueur, and vanilla to egg yolks.

In another clean, large bowl of an electric mixer, beat the egg whites until stiff peaks form but are not dry. Gently fold ¼ of the egg whites into chocolate mixture.

Fold in remaining egg whites until thoroughly incorporated. Pour batter into prepared pan.

Bake for 26 to 35 minutes or until cake is just set. Cool on wire rack.

When completely cool, loosen the edges of the springform pan and remove sides. Serve cake with chunks of fresh pineapple and a wisp of unsweetened whipped cream. Yield: 8 or more servings.

Fresh pineapple and unsweetened whipped cream are perfect complements to something so deep, dark, and delicious.

Chocolate-Chunk Walnut Cake with Black Raspberry Sauce

Chunky textures and surprising flavors in every moist bite, this cake freezes well for a "company's coming!" special treat.

CAKE

- 1½ cups (about 10 oz.) semisweet chocolate, chopped
- 1 cup walnuts, finely ground
- 2 tbsp. plain breadcrumbs
- ½ tsp. baking powder
- 1 cup unsalted butter, room temperature
- 1 cup granulated sugar
- 7 large eggs, separated, room temperature
- 2 tbsp. Frangelico

BLACK RASPBERRY SAUCE

- 1 pint fresh black raspberries, washed, or 2 cups frozen raspberries, thawed
- 2 tbsp. granulated sugar
- 1 tbsp. Framboise or Chambord

Unsweetened whipped cream, for serving

Bev's Bites

Note that once the cake is removed from the oven, it will immediately shrink away from the pan's sides and form wrinkles on top . . . this is homemade character!

If making the Black Raspberry Sauce ahead, chill until needed.

For the Cake: Heat oven to 350 degrees. Butter a 10" springform pan. Line the bottom of the pan with parchment paper, then butter the paper and flour the entire pan.

Combine the chocolate, walnuts, breadcrumbs, and baking powder in a medium bowl. Stir to mix thoroughly, then set aside.

Cream the butter in the large mixing bowl of an electric mixer. Add the sugar and blend until creamy. Scrape down the sides of the bowl and beater.

Add the egg yolks to the butter mixture one at a time and blend thoroughly. Add the Frangelico and blend.

Stir the chocolate mixture into the butter mixture. Set aside.

In a separate, clean bowl of an electric mixer, beat the egg whites until soft peaks form. Gently stir ¼ of the whites into the batter.

Fold remaining whites into the batter until thoroughly combined. Pour batter into prepared pan and bake for 50 to 55 minutes or until a toothpick inserted into the center comes out clean. Place pan on wire rack to cool.

When cake is cool, loosen the edges of the springform pan and remove sides. Quickly and carefully invert the cake onto a plate, remove the pan bottom and parchment paper, and reinvert the cake onto a serving dish or cutting board.

For the Black Raspberry Sauce: Place the raspberries, sugar, and liqueur into the container of a Vitamix blender. Secure lid, then select Variable 1. Slowly increase speed to Variable 10, then High, and blend for 30 seconds or until smooth. Transfer contents to a fine sieve set over a medium bowl and press mixture to extract as much of the sauce as possible while leaving the gritty seeds behind.

When ready to serve, slice a thin piece of cake and place on a serving plate drizzled with some of the Black Raspberry Sauce. Place a dollop of freshly whipped cream on the side and serve immediately. Yield: 8 or more servings.

*Your guests will be suitably impressed with this cake's rich taste—
no need to tell them it wasn't difficult!*

Velvety White Chocolate Truffle Tart with Raspberries

A truly elegant chocolate dessert.

CRUST

1 cup unbleached, all-purpose flour
½ cup confectioners' sugar, sifted
½ cup unsalted butter, cold, cut into pieces
½ tsp. vanilla extract
¼ tsp. almond extract

FILLING

½ cup heavy whipping cream
9 oz. white chocolate, finely chopped
3 tbsp. almond-flavored liqueur or almond syrup for coffee

TOPPING

2 cups red raspberries
3 oz. white chocolate, melted
1 ½ tsp. light olive oil

For the Crust: Heat oven to 350 degrees.

Combine the flour, confectioners' sugar, butter, vanilla extract, and almond extract in a food processor. Pulse just until dough begins to hold together. Remove from food processor and press dough into a 9" or 11" tart pan with removable bottom.

Prick dough all over with a fork. Freeze for 30 minutes.

Bake for 15 to 18 minutes or until golden brown. Cool completely on a wire rack.

For the Filling: In a small saucepan, heat cream to a simmer.

Place chocolate in a food processor. With food processor running, carefully pour hot cream over white chocolate. Add almond liqueur and process until smooth.

Pour mixture into a small bowl. Cover and refrigerate 45 minutes to 1 hour or until cool and beginning to thicken. Spread cooled filling in baked tart shell.

For the Topping: Arrange raspberries over the top of the tart.

Mix chocolate and olive oil until well blended and smooth. Drizzle over raspberries.

Refrigerate tart at least 2 hours or up to 1 day before serving. Keep in the refrigerator. Yield: 8 to 10 servings.

Elegant, easy, and impressive—wow!

Fudge Cake with Warm Ganache

A spoon and a mixing bowl make quick work of sheer chocolate nirvana.

FUDGE CAKE

- 1 cup unbleached, all-purpose flour
- ¼ cup plus 2 tbsp. unsweetened cocoa powder, not Dutch process
- ½ tsp. baking soda
- ¼ tsp. salt
- 4 tbsp. unsalted butter, melted and warm
- 1¼ cups light brown sugar, firmly packed
- 2 large eggs, lightly beaten
- 1 tsp. vanilla extract
- ½ cup simmering water

WARM GANACHE

- 8 oz. bittersweet or semisweet chocolate, finely chopped
- 1 cup heavy whipping cream, plus more as needed
- 1 tbsp. granulated sugar

Heat oven to 350 degrees. Lightly grease the bottom of a 9" round cake pan.

In a medium bowl, sift together the flour, cocoa powder, baking soda, and salt. Set aside.

In a large bowl, stir together the butter and brown sugar. Add the eggs and vanilla. Stir until well blended.

Add the flour mixture all at once and stir just until the flour is moistened. Pour the simmering water over the batter, stirring just until the batter is smooth.

Scrape batter into prepared pan. Bake for 25 to 30 minutes or until a toothpick inserted in the center comes out clean. Let cool in the pan on a rack for 10 minutes. Remove cake from pan and let cool completely on the rack, right side up.

For the Ganache: Place the chocolate in a medium bowl. Set aside.

In a small saucepan, bring the heavy cream and granulated sugar to a simmer. Pour the hot cream over the chocolate and whisk gently until the chocolate is completely melted and smooth. If mixture is too thick to spread, add more cream, 1 tablespoon at a time.

Once the cake is cool, set the wire rack over a baking sheet lined with foil. Pour the warm ganache over the cake and use an icing spatula to spread it over the top of the cake and down the sides. Let set for 2 hours before serving. Yield: 6 to 8 servings.

The ultimate chocolate fix!

CELEBRATE WITH CHEF BEV SHAFFER: CREATING A CHOCOLATE DESSERT BUFFET

If you've ever had the experience of trying to decide which dessert to make out of a cookbook, a buffet is the perfect opportunity to sample several treats that you have your eye on. Here are some tips for creating a deliciously memorable dessert buffet.

- Know your numbers. Look at the number of servings per recipe and consider halving those portions for sampling. If a recipe makes 4 to 6 servings, it could provide samples for 8 to 12 people. A good guide is 2 to 3 recipes for 8 to 12 guests, or 4 to 6 recipes for larger gatherings.
- Vary the temperature. Choose a variety of warm, cold, and room-temperature desserts.
- Try new textures. Choose desserts with different textures, from smooth and creamy to tender and light to rich and dense to crisp and crunchy.
- Diversify the menu. Try desserts with different forms, such as layer cakes, pies, mousses, puddings, or tarts. Remember to pick some with toppings and sauces and some without.
- Plan your set-up. Set the buffet on a kitchen island, dining room table, buffet, or sideboard. Use placemats, tablecloths, napkins or decorative fabric to cover the table surface.
- Be creative. Varying the height of the desserts on display adds appetite appeal and visual interest. You can do this by using serving pieces of varying heights, or you can place inverted serving bowls or boxes under the table dressing to create the illusion of tiers.
- Decorate. Add confetti, curled ribbon, fresh flowers, or other decorative items to the buffet area.
- Add extras. Place toppings such as whipped cream, fresh fruit, nuts, and fudge sauce along with its appropriate serving utensil, next to each dessert.
- Facilitate smooth serving. Pre-cut desserts for easy serving. Consider cutting smaller portions to encourage sampling.
- Offer drinks. Serve coffee, hot water for tea, dessert wine and/or liquors, or sparkling waters.
- Make it easy. Arrange plates at the beginning of the buffet and silverware and napkins at the end. This way, guests aren't juggling too many things at once.
- Treat yourself. Don't forget to enjoy your guests and your desserts!

BIBLIOGRAPHY

Corriher, Shirley O. *BakeWise*. New York: Scribner, 2008.

González, Elaine. *The Art of Chocolate*. San Francisco: Chronicle Books, 1998.

Herbst, Sharon T. *Food Lover's Companion*. 2nd ed. Hauppauge, NY: Barron's Educational Series, 1995.

Shaffer, Bev. *Brownies to Die For!* Gretna, LA: Pelican, 2006.

Shaffer, Bev. *Cakes to Die For!* Gretna, LA: Pelican, 2010.

Shaffer, Bev. *Cookies to Die For!* Gretna, LA: Pelican, 2009.

Shaffer, Bev and John. *No Reservations Required*. Wooster, OH: Wooster Book Company, 2003.

INDEX

Baked Chocolate Espresso Shots, 186
Bev's Bittersweet Chocolate Waffles, 46
Bev's Three-Chocolate Bark with Spiced Pecans and Dried Tart Cherries, 168
Bitter and the (Mostly) Sweet Thumbprint Cookies, The, 59
Bold Chocolate Fudge Cake, 127
Bread and Chocolate: A Little Dessert Bruschetta, 136
Brownie Chunk Cookies, 109
Buttermilk Chocolate Bread with Chocolate Honey Butter, 44

Chicago-Style Deep-Dish Dessert Pizza, 124
Chocolate and Coconut Cream Fondue, 130
Chocolate and More Chocolate Mini Cupcakes, 110
Chocolate Banana Praline Soufflé, 71
Chocolate Blackout Cookies, 129
Chocolate-Caramel Drizzled Oranges, 93
Chocolate Caramels, 149
Chocolate-Caramel Tart with Drunken Raspberries and Whipped Cream, 101
Chocolate Casserole, 54
Chocolate Chip Biscuits with Mangoes and Pineapple, 94
Chocolate Chip Cookie Dough Cheesecake, 142
Chocolate Chip Pumpkin Cheesecake with Chocolate-Cookie Crust, 95
Chocolate Chocolate Chipotle Fudge Milkshake, 56
Chocolate Chocolate Cocoa Cookies, 60
Chocolate-Chunk Walnut Cake with Black Raspberry Sauce, 212
Chocolate Coconut Candy Bars, 160
Chocolate-Covered Almond Butter Crunch, 155
Chocolate Cranberry Oat Cookies, 32
Chocolate Crème Brûlée, 195
Chocolate Crumb-Crusted Chocolate-Caramel Cheesecake, 50
Chocolate Cupcakes with Chocolate Fudge Frosting, 38
Chocolate Fettuccine with Whipped Cream and Fudge Sauce, 126

Chocolate 'Mallow 'Wiches, 114
Chocolate Mousse-Filled Chocolate Cream Puffs, 177
Chocolate-Mousse Filled Meringue Pie, 176
Chocolate Nut Tart, 31
Chocolate Orange Pots de Crème, 180
Chocolate-Orange Sorbet, 76
Chocolate Pavlova, 203
Chocolate Peanut Butter Ice Cream Pie with Chocolate-Cookie Crust, 133
Chocolate Pepita Shortbread Stars, 90
Chocolate Sauce, 158, 199
Chocolate Sorbet, 134
Chocolate Soup with Fruit Salsa or Toasted Nuts, 196
Chocolate Spice Route and Macadamia Tart, 192
Chocolate Sushi, 113
Chocolate Truffles with Flavor Variations, 162
Chocolate-upon-Chocolate Layer Cake with White Chocolate Curls, 120
Chocolate Walnut Fudge, 172
Chocolate-with-a-Hint-of-Orange Bread Pudding, 98
Cocoa-Buttermilk Cake with Cocoa-Mascarpone Frosting, 64
Comforting Collection of Sauces, A, 37
Cracked-Top Chocolate Torta, 189
Crazy Chocolate Cobbler with Seasonal Fresh Fruit, 77
Creamy, Rich Chocolate-Marshmallow Fudge, 156
Crisp Chocolate Biscotti, 152
Crispy Chocolate Snaps, 40

Decadent White Chocolate Pastry Cream, 200
Deep Dark Chocolate Truffle Cake, 210
Downsized Chocolate Decadence, 202
Downsized Turtle Pecan Pie, 132

Favorite Flavors (Chocolate and Raspberry) Layered Cheesecake, 79
Fleur de Sel Dark Chocolate Caramel Truffles, 165
Four-Ways-with-Chocolate Tiramisu, 185
Fudge Cake with Warm Ganache, 216

Fudge Cake with Warm Ganache and Raspberry Jam Topping, 100
Fudge Nut Deep-Dish Pie, 63
Fudge Pudding Cake, 54
Fudgy Brownie Mix, 146
Fudgy Brownies with Chocolate-Cinnamon Mousse, 99
Fudgy Goes Latin Bars, 92

Geraldine's Devil's Food Cupcakes with White Chocolate Espresso Topping or White Chocolate Lemon Topping, 118
Gluten-Free Swirled Brownie Cheesecake Squares, 52
Gooey Caramel Pecan Brownies, 34

Heavenly Homemade Chocolate Marshmallows, 167
Hint-of-Chocolate Cupcakes with Truffle Cream Topping, A, 123
Holiday Chocolate Drops, 145
Hot Chocolate: Comfort in a Cup, 48
How to Make a Truffle Sampler, 161

Individual Chocolate Soufflés, 198
Individual Hot Chocolate Cakes, 41

Java Jolt Chocolate Sandwich Cookies, 206
Jumbo Double-Fudge Brownie Muffins, 140

Kid in All Adults Marshmallow Truffles, The, 164

Light Lemon-Raspberry Cake with White Chocolate Frosting, 72
Live and Let Chai Pots de Crème, 82
Loaded Chocolate-Pecan Coffee Cake, 57

Macaroon Tarts with Chocolate Cream, 194
Mascarpone Chocolate Fondue, 204
Melt-in-Your-Mouth Chocolate Almond Wafers, 184
Mini Chocolate Turnovers, 139
Mocha Cupcakes with White Chocolate Cream Cheese Drizzle, 66
Mocha Fondue, 130

Naked Chocolate Macaroons, 188
Not-Just-for-Tree-Huggin'-Hippies Chocolate Granola, 47
Not My Momma's Rice Pudding with Cranberry Compote, 33

Oh, You Bittersweet Truffle Tart, 178

Panna Cotta Chocolate Layer Cake Banded with Chocolate, 116
Peanut Butter and Chocolate Fondue, 131
Peanut Butter Fudge Brownies, 75

Red, White, and Chocolate Holiday Tart, 104
Rich, Chocolaty, Crème Fraîche Cupcakes, 53

Shaken or Stirred? Chocolatini, 128
Simply Sublime Double-Chocolate Pudding, 42
Slice 'N Bake Chocolate Cookies, 36
Sour Cream Chocolate Layer Cake with Whipped Chocolate Cream Frosting or Milk Chocolate Frosting, 137
Specks-of-Cranberry White Chocolate Yogurt Cheesecake, 80
Stackable Chocolate-Cookie Hearts, 170
Strawberry Sauté, 77
Sumptuous White Chocolate and Brie Cheesecake, 175
Swirls-of-Chocolate Meringues, 181

Triple Chocolate Biscotti, 150
Triple Chocolate Pudding, 209
Triple-Decker Chocolate Cookies, 182

Velvety White Chocolate Truffle Tart with Raspberries, 214

Warm Chocolate Beignets, 55
Warm Chocolate Raspberry Pudding Cake, 86
White Chocolate and Raspberry Bread Pudding with White Chocolate Sauce and a Raspberry Sauce, 102
White Chocolate Bread Pudding with White Chocolate Sauce, 43
White Chocolate Chocolate Biscotti, 89
White Chocolate Coeur à la Crème with Chocolate-Covered Espresso Beans, 190
White Chocolate Mango Bread Pudding with Vanilla Ice Cream and Jane's Butterscotch Sauce, 85
White Chocolate Mousse Tart with Fresh Blueberry Topping, 96
White Chocolate Mousse with Strawberry Coulis, 201